NOLO *Your Legal Companion*

"*In Nolo you can trust.*" —**THE NEW YORK TIMES**

OUR MISSION
Make the law as simple as possible, saving you time, money and headaches.

Whether you have a simple question or a complex problem, turn to us at:

NOLO.COM

Your all-in-one legal resource

Need quick information about wills, patents, adoptions, starting a business—or anything else that's affected by the law? **Nolo.com** is packed with free articles, legal updates, resources and a complete catalog of our books and software.

NOLO NOW

Make your legal documents online

Creating a legal document has never been easier or more cost-effective! Featuring Nolo's Online Will, as well as online forms for LLC formation, incorporation, divorce, name change—and many more! Check it out at **http://nolonow.nolo.com**.

NOLO'S LAWYER DIRECTORY

Meet your new attorney

If you want advice from a qualified attorney, turn to Nolo's Lawyer Directory—the only directory that lets you see hundreds of in-depth attorney profiles so you can pick the one that's right for you. Find it at **http://lawyers.nolo.com.**

ALWAYS UP TO DATE

***Sign up for* NOLO'S LEGAL UPDATER**

Old law is bad law. We'll email you when we publish an updated edition of this book—sign up for this free service at nolo.com/legalupdater.

***Find the latest updates at* NOLO.COM**

Recognizing that the law can change even before you use this book, we post legal updates during the life of this edition at **nolo.com/updates**.

***Is this edition the newest?* ASK US!**

To make sure that this is the most recent edition available, just give us a call at **800-728-3555**.

(Please note that we cannot offer legal advice.)

NOLO

COOPERATIVE LIBRARY SERVICES
Member of Washington County
Beaverton, OR 97005
BEAVERTON CITY LIBRARY

Please note

We believe accurate, plain-English legal information should help you solve many of your own legal problems. But this text is not a substitute for personalized advice from a knowledgeable lawyer. If you want the help of a trained professional—and we'll always point out situations in which we think that's a good idea—consult an attorney licensed to practice in your state.

Retire—And Start Your Own Business

By Dennis J. Sargent & Martha S. Sargent

First Edition	APRIL 2008
Editor	SHAE IRVING
Cover & Book Design	SUSAN PUTNEY
Proofreading	ROBERT WELLS
CD-ROM Preparation	ELLEN BITTER
Index	ELLEN SHERRON
Printing	DELTA PRINTING SOLUTIONS, INC.

Sargent, Dennis J., 1954-
Retire-and start your own business : five steps to success / by Dennis J. Sargent and Martha S. Sargent. -- 1st ed.
p. cm.
ISBN-13: 978-1-4133-0765-8 (pbk.)
ISBN-10: 1-4133-0765-5 (pbk.)
1. New business enterprises. 2. Retirement income. 3. Small business--Management. 4. Success in business. I. Sargent, Martha S., 1947- II. Title.
HD62.5.S2768 2008
658.1'1--dc22
2007047040

Quantity sales: For information on bulk purchases or corporate premium sales, please contact the Special Sales Department. For academic sales or textbook adoptions, ask for Academic Sales. 800-955-4775, Nolo, 950 Parker Street, Berkeley, CA 94710.

Acknowledgments

We first envisioned this book in the spring of 2004. It has expanded and shrunk, absorbed every waking hour and languished on a shelf, been a source of frustration and delight. In the end, we believe it achieves our goal: to help retirees and future retirees choose the right retirement business. We could not have achieved that goal without help and support from many people.

Many thanks to our friends and family who traveled with us through this process; their encouragement and willingness to listen never flagged. Special thanks to Pat Newport and Cheryl McLean for enthusiasm and expert advice at just the right moment, and to Sharon Ross and Judy Beebe for excellent feedback on some of the exercises in this book.

We were thrilled that this project was adopted by Nolo, a publisher we have long admired. And now we know why their books are so respected. From our designer Susan Putney, CD-ROM producer Ellen Bitter, proofreader Robert Wells, to a great marketing staff, Nolo's hard working experts helped make this book professional and successful. Thanks also to Tamara Traeder (formerly Acquisitions Editor for Nolo) for championing our book and to Janet Portman (Managing Editor) and the Nolo editorial department for believing in our book and sticking with us.

Our most sincere thanks to our editor, Shae Irving. With her insights, questions, and knack for simplifying the complex, she transformed our jumble of ideas and information into this book. We have greatly enjoyed our partnership with her.

Finally, to our parents, Frank (deceased) and Kaye Sargent, Joe and Shirley Regan—our successes have always been a tribute to your love and support.

About the Authors

Dennis Sargent retired in December 2006 from his position as Director of the Small Business Development Center (SBDC) at Linn-Benton Community College in Albany, Oregon. In his 24 years with the SBDC, he counseled hundreds of aspiring and established small business owners and taught seminars on many business topics, from starting a business to profit improvement. He is the primary author of *Your Business Plan*, now in its fifth edition, with nationwide sales of over 100,000 copies. Dennis is a former Certified Public Accountant and earned his Masters of Science in Business at Oregon State University.

Martha Sargent retired after an enjoyable career as a professor of business administration, including 20 years at Western Oregon University, where she was recognized for excellence in teaching. She specialized in accounting but also developed and taught in the university's entrepreneurship program. She is a former Certified Public Accountant and Certified Management Accountant and received her MBA from Oregon State University.

Since retiring from their jobs in education, Martha and Dennis divide their time between homes in Redmond, Oregon and Sun City West, Arizona. They're pleased to be living a life that balances their retirement business—teaching and writing—with travel, hiking, golf, photography, and other favorite activities.

Table of Contents

Your Retirement Business Companion

These days, the decision to retire from your job is as much about beginnings as it is about endings. Perhaps you're happy to say goodbye to a job that no longer engages you or a commute that's become a grind. Or, maybe you've suffered an injury or fallen prey to corporate downsizing and you're feeling pressed to retire. In any case, you're probably thinking a lot about what comes next—looking forward to starting new, fulfilling work (paid or unpaid) and reconnecting with interests and people you just haven't had time for.

Millions of Americans see leaving their jobs as the perfect time to grow and prosper by opening their own businesses. Finally, it's your turn to be the boss.

What do you want from your retirement? If you see yourself in one or more of the following descriptions, opening a business could be just the thing to do:

- You've been doing the same job for years and are itching to try something new.
- You've got a business idea that you've always wanted to test.
- You want to be your own boss and do things your way.
- You want to stay active and keep working.
- You'll want some extra income after you retire.

If you want to start a rewarding and successful retirement business, you must choose the right one. We wrote this book to help you do just that, using five straightforward steps.

Step One: Focus on yourself. The process starts with you: what you want to do in retirement, what you value in life, where you want to live. Your answers to these questions are the keys to balancing work and play—and making the next phase of your life as satisfying as you've dreamed it could be.

Step Two: Inventory your resources. We'll help you take stock of the many resources available for your new business—skills, time, and money—so that you can choose the best venture for you.

Step Three: Generate great business ideas. If you want to work for yourself, but you come up empty when trying to decide what kind of business to start, there's no need to worry. We show you lots of ways to find exciting business ideas.

Step Four: Choose your best business idea. Your best business idea will be in alignment with your retirement vision and capable of providing the income you need. We'll walk you through a series of reality checks to make sure you've picked a winner.

Step Five: Get ready to launch your business. Once you've got a great business idea in hand, we'll help you get ready to start. You'll need to be familiar with some basics for small business owners: legal issues, how to finance your business and write a sound business plan, how to handle income taxes and find good health insurance. The last part of this book introduces you to each of these important topics and provides lots of resources to help you get your business going.

Starting a business can be the cornerstone of a great retirement. And you can do it! This book and accompanying CD-ROM are packed with carefully designed tools and resources to guide you along the way. So grab a pencil and settle into your chair, or pull up to your computer and insert the CD-ROM. It's time to get ready to launch that next great adventure in your life: your retirement business.

About This Book

To find out what one is fitted to do, and to secure an opportunity to do it, is the key to happiness.

—JOHN DEWEY

Make no mistake about it: Retirement is a whole new ballgame. Your daily routine, your self-image, your financial situation, the amount of time you spend with your family and friends—it's all going to change. No matter what shape your retirement years will take, your goal should be to make them as fulfilling as possible.

You're reading this book, so you're at least thinking about joining the millions of retirees running their own businesses. One AARP study found that more than 16% of workers aged 50 and older are self-employed. That's 5.6 million people. And one-third of those workers became self-employed after turning 50.

You could be one of them. The key to success is choosing the right retirement business for you.

Why We Wrote This Book

Ever read a book that changed your life? That happened to us many years ago when we read *The Three Boxes of Life and How to Get Out of Them*, by Richard Bolles, acclaimed author of *What Color Is Your Parachute?* (both published by Ten Speed Press). The *Three Boxes of Life* has influenced us ever since and is a big part of why we started our own retirement business and wrote this book.

Bolles asserts that we view our lives in three periods (boxes)—learning, working, and playing. When we're young, we focus on learning. Then, we enter the workforce. And, boy, do we work. Finally, we retire and it's time to play. While we're living in one box, we spend little time or energy on the other two. But Bolles proposes more balance, so that we learn, work, and play in every phase of our lives.

You might argue there are more or fewer boxes than learning, working, and playing. But, no matter how you dice it, the key is balance.

As we thought about leaving our jobs, the three boxes of life took on new importance. How would we build "working" into our retirement lives?

Martha first tried selling real estate and lasted six months before tossing in the towel. The financial rewards were there, but the time commitment and skills required weren't a good match for her. She realized that she hadn't considered some very important factors when choosing her business. If only she'd had this book to read first!

In the meantime, in his capacity as director of a Small Business Development Center, Dennis noticed more and more Baby Boomers seeking his professional advice about starting a retirement business. He developed a seminar to help them—and that seminar grew into this book.

Now we've started another retirement business, training people to pass the Oregon construction contractors licensing exam. It successfully fills the "work" box of our retirement lives. It fits our skills as educators, requires just the amount of time we wish to devote, and turns a profit that works well with our financial goals. We used the process in this book to choose the right retirement business for us—which is exactly what we want to help you do, too.

How This Book Works

You'll find lots of information in this book about starting a retirement business, but we're not just giving you a pile of pages to read. This book is for you to use.

The Tools

Each chapter includes easy-to-use, thought-provoking, practical Tools to help you choose and get ready to launch your successful retirement business. You can use these Tools in several ways:

Write in your book. Some Tools ask you to rank your preferences or circle things important to you. Others give you space to write out an answer. You can do all of this right in your book.

Print from the CD-ROM. You might want to print some of the Tools from the CD-ROM at the back of the book and write on the printouts. This can work well if you want to use the Tool even when your book isn't handy. You'll find instructions on how to do this in Appendix A.

Work directly on computer files. You can save the CD-ROM files to your computer and work on them there. This may be particularly useful in a couple of cases. First, there may be times when you want to add space to a Tool to accommodate additional information. Working with a Tool on your word processor gives you the flexibility to expand it as needed. Second, you might want to work with your computer when you evaluate your financial resources in Chapter 6. We've included *Excel* spreadsheets on the CD-ROM that can do some of the mathematical calculations for you and let you play "what if" with different scenarios. You'll find instructions on how to use these spreadsheets in Appendix A.

We think you'll learn a great deal about yourself and your potential business if you use our Tools, whether you do so on paper or in your head, in great detail or in broad strokes. The key is simply to use them.

The Profile

The first six chapters in this book help you complete your Retirement Business Profile (for the sake of simplicity, we usually call it your "Profile"). Your Profile summarizes your interests, goals, values, work style, and other factors you'll use when choosing your best business idea. The Profile also summarizes the amount of time you plan to put into your business and your financial requirements; you'll need this information when it's time to see whether your chosen business idea really makes sense.

As you work through this book, we let you know when it's time to pause and complete a section of your Retirement Business Profile. You'll find it at the back of the book in Appendix B (if you want to work by hand) and on the CD-ROM (if you want to use your computer to fill it out).

The Steps

There are five steps in the process of choosing your best retirement business. You can work through them from beginning to end or move around as suits your needs.

Step 1: Focus on Yourself

Your best business idea is one that matches what you want to do in retirement and aligns with how you want to do it.

- **Chapter 1** starts the process by helping you think about your interests, from ping-pong to parasailing, carpentry to car repair. Your interests can be a great source of business ideas. Then, to make sure your retirement days are fulfilling, we give you an easy goal-setting process to follow.
- **Chapter 2** helps you explore your values and your work style. Your best chance for success comes if you choose a business that's in agreement with what's important to you and how you think things ought to be done.
- **Chapter 3** adds the final piece for this step—where you want to live in retirement. This can be a big factor in finding a retirement business. You might need to consider local competition for your product or service. Or, you might need to choose a portable business—one that can move around the country with you.

At the end of each chapter in this step, you'll complete part of your Profile to summarize your thoughts.

Step 2: Inventory Your Resources

Step 2 shows you how to inventory three things you'll take with you into your retirement business: your skills, your time, and your money. Taking stock of these resources can make it easier to look for business ideas, choose the one that fits you best, then check to see if it's feasible.

- **Chapter 4** gives you a simple process to inventory your skills, which can be a great source of business ideas. You'll look at all the skills you've acquired, not just through formal education and training, but from all of your experiences—from raising a family to working, playing, traveling, and volunteering.

- **Chapter 5** is about deciding how you want to spend your time in retirement. It's important that you consider how much time you wish to put into your business and into all the other things you want to do. That way, you can choose a business that fits.
- **Chapter 6** is all about money—how much money you have available to start your business, and how much income you want to get out of it. The chapter includes easy-to-understand Tools to help you inventory your financial resources, including any income you expect from retirement plans, Social Security, real estate, and investments. You'll also list the expenses you expect to incur and put it all together in a sensible financial summary.

You'll add your Step 2 inventory to your Profile—and you'll be one step closer to choosing the right retirement business for you.

Step 3: Generate Great Business Ideas

Most of us need a little help coming up with business ideas, so that's the third step in our process. We show you how to look often and look everywhere to generate lots of business ideas. That way, you have a better chance of finding the right one for you.

- **Chapter 7** discusses different types of businesses you could start, including retail, wholesale, manufacturing, and service businesses. Considering many options can help you generate more and better ideas.
- **Chapter 8** shows you how to take your search a step further by developing business ideas from your worklife, interests, skills, and experiences as a consumer. We also discuss how following trends in the marketplace can lead to good business ideas.

You'll probably find that the more you look for business ideas, the more exciting ones you find. So we'll give you a handy method to keep track of your ideas.

Step 4: Choose Your Best Business Idea

Once you've got a stack of good business ideas, you need to pick out your best bet.

- **Chapter 9** helps you compare your business ideas to your Profile. You'll use an easy rating system to select your number one business idea.
- **Chapter 10** will show you how to take a close look at your favorite idea to see whether it makes sense. You'll complete four reality checks that help you determine:
  - how many customers you'll need to serve in order to make the money you want to make
  - whether you'll have the time, space, equipment, and materials to serve that many customers
  - who else is running your type of business and whether you'll be able to compete, and
  - how much money it will take to get started and whether you can finance your business.

Your business idea may sound great, but you won't want to launch it unless it passes each reality check.

Step 5: Get Ready to Launch Your Business

After you've completed the previous four steps, you'll have your number one business idea and you'll probably be excited to get going on it. But first, you'll have to prepare.

This final step helps you get ready to start your business. We cover basic information for starting a small business, give you plenty of resources for learning more, and provide simple methods for keeping track of what you need to do.

- **Chapter 11** covers the legal matters you'll need to address, like which form of ownership you'll use, what zoning regulations might apply to your business location, and how you'll protect your creative ideas. You might be able to handle some of these legal matters yourself; for others, you may wish to consult a lawyer. In either case, the more you know about the subject, the easier (and cheaper) it will be to get things done.

- **Chapter 12** discusses options for financing your business. Some businesses require more start-up funds than others, but it's not likely you can get your business off the ground for nothing. You may be like most business owners and use only your own money. Or, you may need to borrow. You'll explore the possibilities and learn about getting a loan if you need one.
- **Chapter 13** gives you the basics about taxes —not just income taxes, but property taxes, sales taxes, and payroll taxes. You'll learn about the self-employment tax, quarterly estimated tax payments you may have to make, and how your Social Security benefits may be taxed.
- **Chapter 14** helps you learn about your options for health insurance—a primary retirement concern for most people. We discuss the basics, give you lots of resources for further exploration, and include a Tool to help you organize your search for the best coverage.
- **Chapter 15** supports all of your efforts by pointing you toward help when you need it. We list self-help books, software, and websites and give you suggestions for finding the best lawyers, accountants, and small business advisers.

Focus on Yourself

Perhaps you spent your working years with one company—or doing the same type of job. If you're like many people, your career path may not have been a conscious choice. It may seem that your work just happened, and when pressed you can't really remember how you ended up with 27 years in the food processing industry and can't honestly say that you are now, or ever were, truly interested in jams and jellies.

When you start your own retirement business, you have the opportunity to be more selective. You can build your business around what you want to do—and you can decide how you want to do it. This first step gets you started by helping you answer three essential questions:

- What do you want to do with your retirement years?
- What is most important to you?
- Where do you want to live?

In **Chapter 1**, we'll help you explore your interests and we'll show you how to set goals so that what you really want to do takes priority in your new life. Then, in **Chapter 2**, you'll look closely at your values, because knowing what matters most to you is a big part of choosing a satisfying business opportunity. Finally, in the last part of this step, **Chapter 3** helps you decide where you want to live out your grand new adventure.

You will summarize your thoughts about each of these topics in your Retirement Business Profile, which you'll later use to generate lots of business ideas and select your best bet.

If this all sounds a bit overwhelming or too time-consuming, you can relax. The Tools are short and sweet, and we'll guide you through each one. They're thought provoking and never boring. Besides, this process is all about you—your interests, your values, your motivations. When's the last time you paid much attention to what's most important to you? Now's your chance.

CHAPTER

1

What Do You Want to Do in Retirement?

Nothing happens unless first we dream.
—CARL SANDBURG

In this chapter, you will explore your interests, set some goals, and get clear about your motivation for starting your own business. Each of these tasks will help you choose a venture that will thrive and bring you satisfaction in your retirement years.

What Interests You?

If you always do what interests you, at least one person is pleased.
—KATHARINE HEPBURN

Mary Ann worked for 25 years as an engineer and planner for a Fortune 500 company. She no longer felt the drive that once spurred her to excel in her career, and work became draining. She was restless, spending more and more time thinking about what else she could do with her life. When the company downsized and offered a severance package, she was hooked. Mary Ann loves to fish. She took her severance and bought into a fly-fishing store.

To start the process of picking your best business, we encourage you to think about what you like to do now, what has interested you in the past, and what you might want to try in the future. Is there something you've been itching to try that you've never done before? We get caught up in our busy lives and can be too tired—or just too set in our ways—to even think about new activities, let alone pursue them. But the perfect business idea could be hidden in one of your untested interests.

The Tools in this section will help you explore a wide range of subjects and activities, leading to a list of favorites that may reveal the key to your new business. The first Tool is a warm-up exercise, designed to prompt your thinking about what you want to do. Circle any items that interest you. Don't worry about choosing too many things: at the end of the section, you'll have a chance to zero in on what you like best. For now, be expansive. And don't stop with the interests we've included. If you think of something that's not listed here, write it down and circle it.

JUMPSTART YOUR THINKING

Enjoying the beauty of nature	Taking care of animals	Woodworking
Listening to music	Competing in sports	Bowling
Eating good food	Running marathons	Gardening
Playing a musical instrument	Working on cars	Bird-watching
Cooking gourmet meals	Working with numbers	Carpentry
Quilting or sewing	Working with technology	Reading
Collecting rare items	Playing chess	Traveling
Making things by hand	Studying history	Painting
Traditional holiday activities	Making wine	Panning for gold
Natural resource conservation	Political activism	Sailing
Writing stories/poems/music	Glassblowing	Photography
Spiritual growth activities	Law enforcement	Fishing
Home decorating	Caring for children	Investing
Playing computer games	Playing golf	Swimming
Buying/developing land	Home construction	Walking
Fixing things that are broken	Alternative medicine	Yoga
Riding motorcycles	Crossword puzzles	Hiking
Making videos	Product design	Farming
Styling hair	Making jewelry	Playing poker
Doodling	Shopping	Playing softball
Creating stained glass art	Food preserving	Biking
People-watching	Acting	Hunting
Collecting rocks	Weightlifting	Playing tennis
Health care	Inventing new products	Singing
Origami	Archery	Stock-car racing
Astrology	Astronomy	Zoology
Horseback riding	Skiing	Education
Promoting literacy	Community action	Dancing
Building model airplanes	Working at charitable organizations	Learning foreign languages
Learning about other cultures		

You can add to your list of interests and potential business ideas by completing the following exercise. It will help you stretch your thinking about what you might like to do, not only by reminding you of what you used to enjoy, but by considering what you would try if nothing stood in your way. What would you do if you had nothing to fear?

IF YOU COULD DO ANYTHING

If I were 18 again, I would:

____

If money were no object, I would:

____

If I were king/queen for a day, I would:

____

If I had only six months left to live, I would:

____

I really like being with people who:

____

My most enjoyable hours are those spent:

____

I don't do it often anymore, but I used to enjoy:

____

I've seen other people doing this, and I'd really like to try it:

____

My most cherished successes have come when I have been:

____

Whenever I get the chance, I read about:

____

Look over the statements above. Do they make you think of activities that interest you? Write them down below.

____

____

____

While exploring your interests, you might have felt like the kid in the proverbial candy shop, wanting a little bit of everything. And that's just fine. But now you need to winnow your favorite subjects and activities into a list that will help you choose potential retirement businesses. Go back over the last two exercises and ask whether you can see yourself putting time or money into each of the interests you've identified. If your answer is no, cross out that interest area for now. It doesn't mean that interest won't be part of your life, just that it isn't likely to be the source of your best business idea.

> **John and Kathy** retired from their long-held jobs with a metals fabrication company and devoted their attention to one of their passions: growing lavender. They didn't intend to open a business, but their acre of lavender plants attracted attention, and soon they recognized an opportunity. They now sell lavender plants and dried lavender products at farmers markets. It's a seasonal business, which fits perfectly with their goal of traveling to a new country each year.

Write your remaining interests in the box below.

YOUR KEY INTERESTS

These subjects or activities interest me now and I definitely want them to be part of my life in retirement:

____

____

I used to be interested in these subjects or activities. I would like to take them up again in retirement:

____

____

I've never explored these subjects or activities before, but I would love to try them:

____

____

You now have a good list of your interests. Keep it handy—you will come back to it when you complete your Profile and start looking for business ideas.

What Are Your Retirement Goals?

Just think—no more long commutes to work. No more endless meetings, tiresome bureaucracy, or office politics. No more sleepwalking through mundane tasks you've completed so many times you can't remember if they were ever new and exciting. Plenty of people look forward to leaving their jobs.

But maybe you will miss your work. You get a charge out of closing a deal or perfecting a product. You're proud of your craftsmanship and that company management sent every new hire to you to learn from the best. You enjoyed the camaraderie at the office or the challenge of learning new technology.

Whether you approach your retirement with relief or trepidation, one thing is certain: You will leave behind the structure and direction your work provided and will need to build a new routine. If you don't have some good ideas about what to do with your days, you could find that time slips by with little sense of satisfaction. You could find yourself hardly working or working hard without meaningful results.

Marcie worked for 20 years in the administrative offices of a major university. At first, she was glad to give up her job. Retirement gave her time to pay attention to her garden, catch up on reading, and spend more time with friends. But as the months went by, Marcie felt increasingly restless. To stay active and give her days some structure, she and a friend started walking regularly with a national organization that enlists walkers and runners to raise money for charity. The first year, Marcie walked a half-marathon. The next, she met her goal of walking a full marathon. One thing led to another, and eventually Marcie started doing freelance work for the nonprofit group, helping to organize their local office.

Setting goals is a great way to ensure that you live your retirement life purposefully. You will get more enjoyment from your life—and greater success from your business—if you set constructive goals and learn to balance them.

You may have had some negative experiences with goals in your workplace. Perhaps you spent far too many working hours at meetings rehashing company goals that no one seemed to care about, knowing that the latest directive would be distributed in a nice binder only to gather dust on a shelf. Or maybe you received top-down mandates or impossible challenges set by corporate planners who never did your job. But don't shy away from setting goals now—because this time, you're in charge. These goals are all about you. You're going to set attainable goals and use them to successfully establish your retirement business and your retirement life.

If you feel intimidated by the idea of setting clear goals, don't worry. This section will show you how. On the other hand, if you're an expert goal setter, the Tools that follow will help you focus on exactly what you want to accomplish in retirement.

Keep in mind that you'll start by considering the big picture, which may include everything from organizing the garage to auditioning for the next community play. Starting a business is one important goal, but you will view it in the context of everything you'd like to do.

The Anatomy of a Goal

If you're bored with life—you don't get up every morning with a burning desire to do things—you don't have enough goals.

—LOU HOLTZ

Setting goals is a matter of knowing what you want and properly allocating your resources—primarily time and money—to reach your desired ends. To increase your chances of success, you'll want to focus on the attributes of an effective goal statement. Many experts use some variation of the acronym SMART to describe a good goal statement. We've found it helpful to add a little more, so here's a list that's SMARTPLUS:

- **Specific.** The more precise your goals, the more likely you can put them into action. Saying "I will paint more" doesn't give you clear direction or help with resource allocation. But if you say "I will complete an oil painting of my grandmother's family home," you will be more focused and more likely to accomplish your goal.
- **Measurable.** You need a means of measurement to know whether you've accomplished your goal. Some examples: "I will lose 20 pounds." "I will walk three miles five days per week." "I will read one classic per month." But measurement does not necessarily mean quantity. You may meet a travel goal by visiting India, or an education goal by completing a college history class.
- **Attainable.** There is much debate about how difficult it should be to reach your goals. If a goal is too easy, it's not likely to motivate you. If it's too hard, you may give up hope. Only you can decide how to challenge yourself without going overboard.
- **Rewarding.** Achieving your goal should make you feel great. It doesn't matter if anyone else recognizes your achievement, as long as you do. It should be something you really want, not something that someone else thinks you ought to do.
- **Timely.** Without a deadline or time frame for your goal, you're not likely to make much progress. Remember, goal setting involves resource allocation, so whatever's at the top of your list is likely to suck up most of the hours in a day. Setting a time frame for a goal will help to ensure that you spend time on it. This doesn't mean all of your goals must be reached soon. You may have daily goals, monthly goals, and lifetime goals.
- **Positive.** It's usually much more effective to state your goals in a positive way. Athletic coaches know that positive statements are better motivators. You'll likely have more success with "I will keep my head still when I putt" than "I won't look up when I putt." Likewise, you'll have more enthusiasm if you say "I will spend four evenings per week working on my model train refurbishing business" than if you tell yourself "I won't watch so much television in the evening."

- **Linked.** Link your goals to the balance of work, play, and learning you envision in retirement. You can't control everything. Other people, the economy, even the weather may affect what you can and can't do. But to the extent possible, develop goals that support how you want to live in retirement and you will find it easier to stay in control.
- **Unbundled.** If you look carefully at a goal, you'll probably find that it contains subgoals—or smaller steps. If your goal is to run a marathon, you might first set a goal to run a 10K. If you break down your goals in this way, they will be easier to accomplish and you can enjoy the feeling of success along the way.
- **Shifting.** A key to achieving your goals is maintaining focus, but don't think this means your goals are set in stone. Goals can, and do, change. That's why it's important to keep an eye on your progress and consider whether your goals need adjustment. But be careful not to shift a goal just so you can say you accomplished it, or to save face if you've made no progress at all.

I Want To ...

Most people need some time to think about what they want to do in retirement. There are so many possibilities! If you're not sure where to begin, look back at the interest areas you identified and think about where you want to spend your energy. For example, if you listed an interest in stamp collecting, you might decide that you want to increase your collection of commemorative stamps, or join a stamp club, or finally get all your stamps organized and into albums.

SKIP AHEAD

If you know your goals. If you already know what you want to do in retirement, that's terrific. You can move on to the next section, where you will have the opportunity to write effective statements to help you achieve your goals.

You might discover that you want to spend more time with your grandchildren, start exercising regularly, or dust off your flute and play in the local orchestra. You may want to travel to Costa Rica, rebuild the engine in your 1965 Mustang, or bake your own bread. And what about that novel you started writing 20 years ago?

Below, we'd like you to write down all the retirement goals you can think of. There are spaces for ten, but feel free to list more or fewer. Your goals don't have to be in any particular order—in other words, don't prioritize them yet. Don't even be concerned about whether they are SMARTPLUS. You'll refine your goals in the next section.

Don't forget to list that you want to start a business. You don't need to be more specific than that. If you don't know what kind of business you want to start, that's okay. Jot down something general, such as "I want to start a business close to home," or "I want to start a business that has something to do with birding." You will explore your opportunities and set specific business goals in later chapters.

YOUR RETIREMENT GOALS

In retirement, I want to ...

____

____

____

____

____

____

____

____

____

____

Don't Be Stingy When Setting Goals

Be expansive when you imagine what you want to do, including goals in many categories. Consider the following types of goals:

Artistic	Travel	Health
Education	Volunteering	Spiritual
Financial	Serving Others	Work and Business
Recreation	Family	

Writing Effective Goal Statements

Now it's time to make a list of your most important retirement goals, putting them in the form of effective goal statements. Because these goals can affect how you'll spend your retirement resources of time and money, you'll want to express them clearly before you take the next step toward starting your business.

When stating your goals, keep in mind the SMARTPLUS factors discussed above. Your goal statements will be explicit about two very important SMARTPLUS factors: measurement and time.

Here are a few examples to show you how it works:

GOAL: Launch my retirement business

I will know I've met this goal when I sign my first customer contract.

I will accomplish this goal by February 15, 2009.

GOAL: Build a new oak entertainment center

I will know I've met this goal when I've moved the entertainment center into the living room.

I will accomplish this goal within three months.

GOAL: Learn to play the flute

I will know I've met this goal when I can play "Greensleeves."

I will accomplish this goal within two years of retiring.

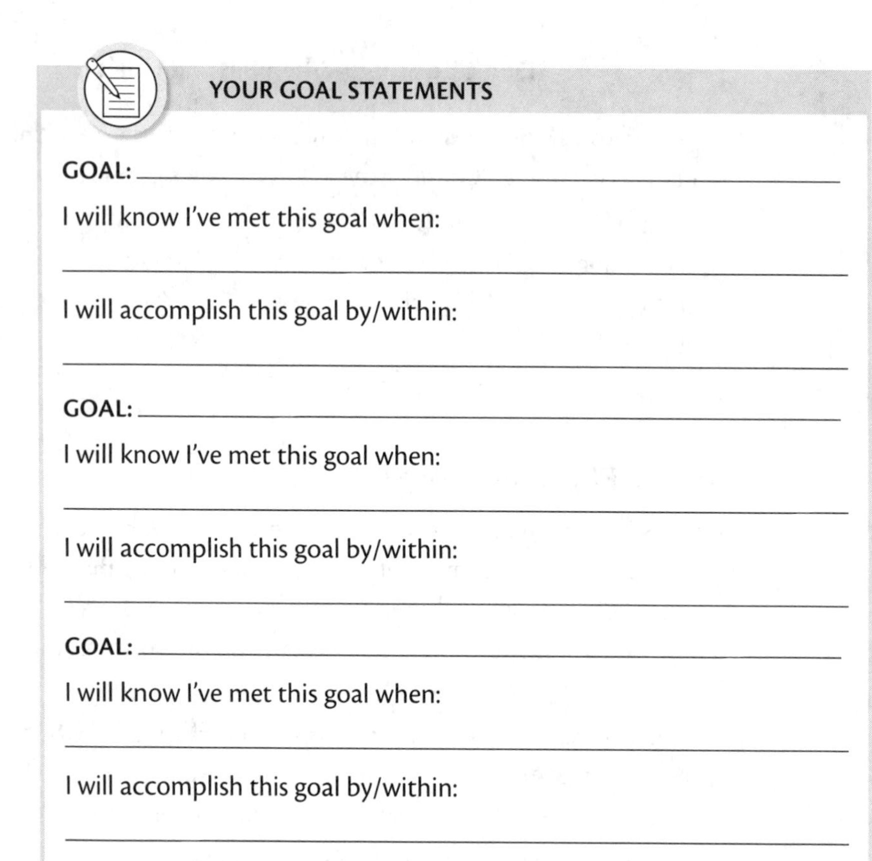
YOUR GOAL STATEMENTS

GOAL: ______________________________

I will know I've met this goal when:

____

I will accomplish this goal by/within:

____

GOAL: ______________________________

I will know I've met this goal when:

____

I will accomplish this goal by/within:

____

GOAL: ______________________________

I will know I've met this goal when:

____

I will accomplish this goal by/within:

____

You now have a good list of your retirement goals. Your goals should be important touchstones as you move forward with the process of choosing and starting your retirement business. Remember to remain focused but flexible: Your goals may shift a bit when you look more closely at how you want to spend your time and how much money you are likely to have. You will explore both of these areas in detail when you take inventory of your resources in Step 2 of this book.

CD-EXTRA!

Accomplish your goals with an action plan. In addition to investing time and money, there may be other steps to take to meet a goal: information to gather, skills to learn, equipment to buy. An action plan is a good way to summarize these details and make a timeline. You can find an action plan and instructions for completing it in the Extras! file on the CD-ROM. You can use an action plan to start accomplishing goals now—and come back to it again after you're ready to start your business, when you'll surely have lots of new goals to master.

TIP

Get Inspired. You'll make more progress toward a goal if you have a daily reminder of what you want to accomplish. Athletes tape photos of championship trophies on their lockers. Dieters post a calorie counter on their refrigerator or hang a favorite too-tight outfit where they can see it. Long before he was famous, the actor and comedian Jim Carrey set a goal of signing a $12 million movie contract. He wrote out a check to himself for $12 million and carried it in his wallet. He more than achieved his goal.

Find something that signifies the successful achievement of your goal and put it where you can see it every day.

Why Do You Want to Start a Business?

Motivation is a fire from within. If someone else tries to light that fire under you, chances are it will burn very briefly.

—STEPHEN R. COVEY

You are reading this book, so one of your goals is starting a business. At the very least, you're thinking about it. Why? Thinking honestly about your motivation—and making sure it's real—will help you make good business choices and head off trouble. For example, you might tell your spouse, "I'm starting this business because I always wanted to grow orchids. I can't wait to sink my hands into some great compost." And maybe this is true. You've always liked flowers and orchids are exotic and enticing. But what if your motivation runs deeper? If you let yourself think about it, perhaps you should also be telling your spouse, "I want to make some extra money from this orchid business. I'm very worried about our income during retirement. What if one of us gets really sick? How would we pay our bills?"

Your motivation for self-employment will most likely influence what your business should be. If your priority is making money, then you'll want to evaluate the profit potential of your business ideas and choose the one that's most likely to give you a great return. If your primary motivation is to do something you're passionate about, and you really could happily lose yourself in a steamy greenhouse, be sure your business lets you follow your dream.

You probably have more than one motivation for starting a retirement business. The following Tool will help you get all of your motivations on the table, ready for contemplation and discussion. Rate each statement on a scale from 1 to 5, where 1 is not at all relevant and 5 is very relevant.

Your rankings should help clarify why you want to start a business in retirement. This, in turn, will help you choose the type of business that's best for you.

YOUR MOTIVATION

I am motivated to start a retirement business because:

- ❑ I've got a business idea I'm really excited about.
- ❑ I need to. My retirement income won't cover my expenses.
- ❑ I'm afraid to have time on my hands. What else would I do with myself?
- ❑ I want the freedom to make my own decisions.
- ❑ I'm not finished using my talents and strengths professionally.
- ❑ I want to be the boss, set my own policies, and make the decisions.
- ❑ I have all these contacts and it's a shame to let them go to waste.
- ❑ If I have to stay around the house for long, I'll get too restless.
- ❑ I like working.
- ❑ I believe I can make a bundle in my business.
- ❑ I want flexibility in what I do with my time.
- ❑ I've never been paid what I'm worth. I'll make more with my own business than I did before retirement.
- ❑ I like winning and I believe I can do this business better than anyone else.

MY PROFILE

Completing Your Profile. Before you start the next chapter, take a few moments to fill out the sections of your Retirement Business Profile that summarize your interests, goals, and motivations. Remember, when your Profile is complete, you'll use it to align your business idea with what is most important to you, ensuring that you're choosing the most successful business for your retirement. You can find the Profile at the back of this book and on the CD-ROM.

CHAPTER

2

What Is Important to You?

It's not hard to make decisions when you know what your values are.
—ROY DISNEY

Just think. Your own business. You can choose a venture that excites you, keeps you motivated, and is run as you've always thought a business should be run. Sure, you will have to answer to customers, suppliers, and any employees you hire. And not many businesses get away with ignoring all traditional business practices. But your business can, and should, reflect your personality and your values.

Defining What Matters

Values are statements of what matters to you. They come from your personal beliefs and goals. If a particular belief or goal is elevated above others in importance, it becomes a value. To describe this process, we like the analogy used by Hyrum W. Smith, business executive, author, and creator of the Franklin Dayplanners.

> **Jeremy** rides his bike ten miles to work, opts for the stairs rather than the elevator, and plays racquetball at noon on Tuesdays and Thursdays. Jeremy values physical fitness. He plans to start a retirement business as a fitness coach for seniors.

It goes like this: Imagine a steel beam, 120 feet long and six inches wide. The beam is lying on the ground, with you standing at one end and your friend at the other. Imagine that your friend reaches into his wallet and pulls out $100. Your challenge: Walk across the beam in less than two minutes and collect the money. Would you do it?

Most people would. So, let's raise the stakes. Imagine two buildings 120 feet apart. The beam now runs between the two buildings, secured just outside the windows on the 38th floor. (If you're terrified of heights, the beam may rest only two flights up, but you get the idea.) You are in one building, your friend in the other. If your friend waves $100, would you walk across the beam to claim it? Probably not. What if he waves $10,000? $100,000? $1,000,000?

Not motivated by money? Imagine instead that your friend holds in his hands the key to inner peace and harmony. Or, perhaps he holds all you'd need to quit work and enter a university doctoral program in your favorite subject. Maybe he holds an abundance of time to spend with family and friends, or financial security, or the chance to tackle something new and challenging. Would you walk across the beam?

Erica cringes every time she passes Greg's office, averting her eyes from the jumble of papers weighted down by greasy pizza boxes and the teetering towers of files. She hurries to her own office and sighs in relief at the sight of the clear desktop and color-coded trays stacked neatly on her credenza. Erica values orderliness and when she starts her retirement business, you can bet everything will be neat and tidy.

That's how you can think about values. Of all your beliefs and goals, which would you cross the beam for?

Listing Your Values

We can tell our values by looking at our checkbook stubs.

—GLORIA STEINEM

From an early age, your values are influenced by the words and behaviors of those around you: Share your toys. Eat everything on your plate. Respect your elders. And your environment continues to shape you as you age. You probably share many values with your family or friends, your culture, members of your religion, or a political group.

Even so, the world reverberates with diversity, and it is unlikely that all of your values agree completely with those of any group. For example, you might share with members of your church the values of honesty, faithfulness, and helping those less fortunate, but it is unlikely you all value solitude, spontaneity, or protecting the environment.

When asked about your own values, you might think only of a few that are obvious to you. But this chapter encourages you to broaden your perspective; an expanded list of values will help you choose and design a successful retirement business.

Below, you'll find a Tool to help you list your values. This process is not intended to influence your values or impose new ones upon you. There are no right or wrong answers. The exercise merely helps you inventory your values so you can use them consciously when it's time to make decisions.

As you consider your values, it may help to think about the interests you listed in the last chapter. For example, let's say you named mountain climbing as an interest. What is it that you value about mountain climbing? Attention to detail? Teamwork? Taking risks?

Or, what if you are interested in quilting? Perhaps one of the things you value about quilting is experimenting with fabrics and colors. Make sure you have "experimenting with fabrics and colors" on your list of values. It could be significant in choosing your retirement business. Your business might not be about quilting, but it might be about fabrics and colors in some other medium—home decorating, clothing design, or developing colorful plush toys.

When stating her values, **Sandy** found it easy enough to scratch the surface. She named honesty, charity, kindness, and family as her primary values. But to support her search for new business ideas, she had to dig a little deeper. She realized that, among other things, she also valued artistic expression and supporting local businesses. This led to the idea that she could open a store to sell locally made handicrafts.

Here's a list a values. Circle any that ring true for you. If a value comes to mind that's not on this list, add it at the bottom and circle it.

YOUR VALUES INVENTORY

Doing as I say I will
Debating all sides of an issue
Competence
Accomplishing a task
Being organized
Holding power over others
Being able to trust someone
Adrenaline rushes
Keeping in contact with people
Doing the best I can
Helping those less fortunate
Being adventurous
Spontaneity
Inquisitiveness
Romance
Joking around
Conformity
Dreaming up new ideas
Creating beauty
Helping other people excel
Mastering a new subject
Financial security
Finishing what I start
Having choices
Being a leader
Devotion
Intimacy
Diving in to solve new problems
Empowering others
Protecting the environment
Working with colors

Thrill of competition
Cheerfulness
Things that challenge me
Self-responsibility
Working with my hands
Being in control
Variety/change
Being on time
Cleanliness
Treating others fairly
Taking time to think
Bravery
Calm
Spirituality
Openness
Looking my best
Dedication
Staying healthy
Giving to others
Being professional
Democracy
Solitude
Perfection
Authenticity
Planning ahead
Making a contribution
Safety
Quiet time
Being the life of the party
Integrity
Expression through music

Dependability
Intelligence
Politeness
Being independent
Being frugal
Precision
Loyalty
Ambition
Learning
Being honest
Taking risks
Thoughtfulness
Creativity
Gratitude
Having fun
Keeping fit
Faithfulness
Honor
Peace
Justice
Holistic living
Trust
Education
Vitality
Orderliness
Being of service
Power
Wealth
Abundance
Excellence
Coordinating

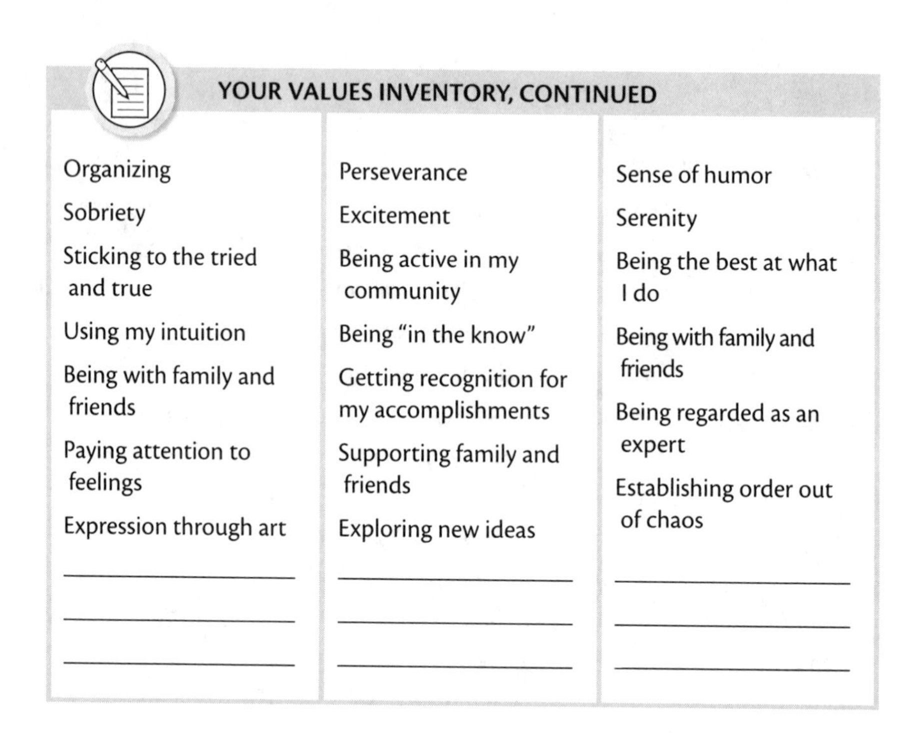

YOUR VALUES INVENTORY, CONTINUED

Organizing	Perseverance	Sense of humor
Sobriety	Excitement	Serenity
Sticking to the tried and true	Being active in my community	Being the best at what I do
Using my intuition	Being "in the know"	Being with family and friends
Being with family and friends	Getting recognition for my accomplishments	Being regarded as an expert
Paying attention to feelings	Supporting family and friends	Establishing order out of chaos
Expression through art	Exploring new ideas	
____________	____________	____________
____________	____________	____________
____________	____________	____________

Self-Image as a Value

Many retirees feel a loss of identity when they leave their employment. Our society is very work oriented and, for better or for worse, we tend to define ourselves by our occupation or our employer. I am a plumber. I am a teacher. I sell vacuums. I work for IBM.

For some, taking on the new title of "retiree" works just fine. It can even be a source of pride. But, for others, "retiree" signifies being over-the-hill, out-of-the-loop, a has-been. This type of identity crisis is especially difficult if you value the image or prestige you used to enjoy while working.

Starting a retirement business might help ease any loss of identity you feel, but only if you get the same sense of pride from your business as you did from your job. That's an example of why it's important to honestly state your values and choose a business that reflects them.

Zeroing In on Your Priorities

By definition, a value is something you care about, but you probably feel stronger about some of your values than others. As with your interests, winnowing your values to a list of what matters most will help you focus when you're considering business ideas. Some of the values you circled above may sound good, but do they really inspire you to spend your time, money, or effort?

We suggest that you review the values you circled and select a maximum of six that are most important to you. You can write them in the blanks below, along with six second-tier values and six values that come in third.

YOUR KEY VALUES

Priority Values:

____

____

____

Second-Tier Values:

____

____

____

Third-Tier Values:

____

____

____

Ranking your values can help you decide how to put them to work in your business and in your life. For instance, you might want a priority value to be at the core of your business. You might build your business around your strongly held value of environmental protection: selling environmentally friendly products or consulting on energy efficiency. Or, if environmental protection is a second-tier value for you, you may want it to be part of how your business operates, even though it's not your core product or service: a window washing service using biodegradable soaps and reducing water usage, or a hairstylist using only natural, nontoxic shampoos and conditioners.

Some of your values might be expressed in other areas of your life and not your business. Maybe you will express your value of caring for animals by donating time to the humane society, but your business will have nothing to do with animals. Take a careful look at your top values, above. Does any one of them call out to you as the potential key to your business?

What's Your Work Style?

Our character is what we do when we think no one is looking.

—H. JACKSON BROWN, JR.

Some values directly influence the way you like to work—your work style, if you will. Thinking about what's important to you in these areas will be of great benefit in setting up your business. This section helps you reflect on four important aspects of your work style:

- your need for social contact
- your ability to motivate yourself and get things done
- your level of comfort with change and transition, and
- whether you tend to focus on details or the big picture.

You'll find a Tool at the end of this section to help you gauge where you stand on each issue.

Social Contact

Solitude is as needful to the imagination as society is wholesome for the character.

—JAMES RUSSELL LOWELL

It happens every afternoon. One person drifts over to the coffee station. A second follows. Soon, most of the staff has gathered to fill their cups and swap stories about the work day. You won't believe this … you should have seen it … did you hear about … ?

Does this sound like you? Or are you the one who often skips the social gatherings to focus on the task at hand? An important part of choosing your new business is deciding how much time you want to spend with others—and who you would like them to be.

How Much Contact Do You Want?

Let's say you've just put down the phone after receiving a huge contract. Yes! You spin around in your chair, pump both fists in the air. Yes! You jump up and take two giant steps to the office door, ready to run down the hall and tell your coworker, Fred, all about it.

But if you're in this business on your own, there is no Fred. Who are you going to call? How will you share this great news?

Some people prefer to work alone. They have little need for coffee-station gatherings and are happy to share their successes and failures with family or friends instead of coworkers. In fact, for them, one of the great things about self-employment is the ability to get away from the office crowd. If that's you, be sure to keep your desire for solitude in mind when choosing your business. Maybe you'd enjoy an online business, with only virtual social contact. Or, perhaps your glass bead jewelry will be sold on consignment at art galleries, letting someone else deal with the customers and giving you more hours alone in your studio.

On the other hand, if you've always reveled in the social connections at your workplace, you will want to choose a retirement business that provides the contact you need. You might consider shared office facilities in a building downtown rather than an isolated office in your home. You might join a support group of business owners. Maybe you'll take your fantastic barbecue sauce on the road, replacing the "old gang" at the office with the "new gang" making the rounds at fairs and festivals.

To Network or Not?

Your business is going to need customers, but there are countless ways to find them. Many service businesses rely heavily on networking to generate new jobs. If you start a consulting business, you'll spend much of your time meeting potential clients and following up with them until you sign a contract. You might need to attend city council meetings or national conferences. You might need to work trade shows, make cold calls, or ask acquaintances for referrals.

If networking sounds awful to you, then you'd best choose a business that attracts customers in some other way. Perhaps an online business is right for you, or a business for which you already have all the contacts you'll need.

What Type of Contact Do You Want?

It's wise to think about how much social contact you want, but it's just as important to consider whom that contact will be with. Relating to customers is not the same as relating to coworkers, which is not the same as relating to employees or to other business owners. In each interaction, you play a different role. The amount of time you spend together, the topics you can discuss, and the expectations for performance will set the tone for the openness, camaraderie, and give-and-take you enjoy from your business relationships.

Different types of businesses also require different relationships with customers. If your business is to bake and sell gluten-free breads and pastries, your experience with customers will be very different if you sell to local grocery stores than if you open a retail store where folks come in to sip coffee, munch a cookie, and chat with you.

Self-Motivation

Ah, the freedom to be your own boss! Do what you want, when you want, where you want. You don't have to rely on anyone else and no one is looking over your shoulder. Perfect!

But is it?

It's just you. Every decision, every plan, every action comes from you. No one else will make you sit down at that desk or trudge out to the shop and build those birdhouses. Your business may pull you in one direction while your family tugs you in another, and only you can find the balance. And you can't pass the buck because it will come right back again.

Your new venture will place the burden of motivation squarely on your shoulders. The right business should help you manage your new responsibilities. If you choose wisely, you will enjoy what you do most of the time and be so eager to do it that you might have the opposite problem: You might have to discipline yourself to pay attention to other aspects of your life. That said, if self-motivation isn't your strongest suit, maybe you should explore businesses that will require you to work closely with others. Knowing that someone else is counting on you could provide the motivation you need. You may also find it helpful to start a business that requires you to meet regular deadlines.

Whatever you do, don't confuse your new-found freedom with permission to be lazy or disorganized. To succeed, your business will need focus and structure, policies and procedures. So expect some red tape, but know that at least it will be your red tape.

Change and Transition

To change and to change for the better are two different things.
—GERMAN PROVERB

Retirement is a big transition. Starting a business is a big change, too. You plan to do both. How will you deal with it all?

Picture yourself high above the crowd in a big-top circus, swinging on a trapeze. Both hands firmly grip the bar. As you swing forward, an empty bar swings toward you. Are you staring below, hoping to see a net—a really, really big net? Will you cling to the bar in hand until you can safely reach the new bar, and only then let go? Or, will you let go of the bar you are holding and leap to grab the empty bar, oblivious to the long drop below you?

You've probably dealt with change and transition in the same way for as long as you can remember. If you typically stick your big toe in the water and then think carefully about the consequences of submerging yourself, or if you usually jump in feet first without testing the water's temperature, don't expect to act differently in retirement.

There are many ways to transition from your former working life to your retirement business. The one you choose should respect how you deal with change. If change is difficult for you, make your transition into self-employment gradual. Start your business before you actually retire, perhaps working on it ten hours per week. Get to know the industry. Much of what we fear about change is the unknown. You can reduce your fears by becoming knowledgeable while still financially and emotionally secure in your job.

Of course, you might be one of the thousands that face premature retirement, out of a job after a corporate merger, retrenchment, or change in management. Or, early retirement might come after injury. In these cases, you probably won't have enough forewarning to plan the transition into your retirement business. What you do, and how fast you do it, may depend on your financial resources. Even so, it is best to respect your feelings about change and accomplish the transition in a way most comfortable to you.

If you enjoy change and sticking with the same old thing bores you, you'd best pick a business that keeps you on your toes. Of course, every business has routine, boring tasks, and no small business owner can completely avoid them, but you won't be happy in a business in which you perceive more drudgery than excitement. Instead, choose a dynamic business that will keep you intrigued. You might want a business in a field totally different from what you did in your career.

Details v. Big Picture

One shock to most first-time business owners is that they have to spend many hours on tasks they don't want to do. Consider Henry, who started a retirement business as an orchid grower. Pruning, planting, watering, caressing the fabulous plants, those are the tasks to be done, right? Yes, except Henry also has to do the marketing and accounting. For every two hours spent blissfully in the greenhouse, Henry might spend one hour on the phone making sales and arranging delivery, and another hour creating invoices and ordering supplies.

Owning a business is a combination of big-picture strategizing and nuts-and-bolts paper pushing. Most business owners enjoy one more than the other, but it all needs to be done for the business to succeed. Of course, if you truly despise bookkeeping, or if working with numbers makes your palms sweat, you can get help. (You'll learn more about that in Step 5 of this book.) But you're not likely to avoid every task you find unpleasant.

Maybe you revel in details. You like nothing better than to take a disorganized mass of paperwork and turn it into precisely labeled files with a place for everything and everything in its place. If so, then you might seek a retirement business that offers an abundance of detailed work. Perhaps you would enjoy an income tax preparation service, or processing insurance claims, or being a freelance technical editor.

But if too much detailed work bores you to tears, don't select a retirement business that will drown you in forms, lists, rules, and regulations.

Summing Up

The following Tool helps you think about your working style and comfort level when it comes to social contact, self-motivation, change, and work duties.

This is a great Tool to do with your spouse, a friend, or a small group of supporters who will give you honest feedback. How you see yourself and how others see you are not always the same. The instructions below assume more than one participant, but feel free to do the Tool alone. Remember, as with every Tool in this book, there are no good, bad, right, or wrong answers.

Make a copy of the Tool for each person participating. (Use a photocopier or print multiple copies from the CD-ROM at the back of the book.) The Tool contains five continuums. Where do you fit on each one? Mark the spot with a pen or pencil. Your supporters should mark their copies with where they see you as well. (You also can do this with each person marking where they see themselves and where they see each other. Use initials or different colored pens for this.) After each participant has marked the continuums, compare and discuss the results.

YOUR WORK STYLE

When it comes to social contact:

I much prefer to be by myself or with just a few other people.	I love being around other people. The more the merrier.

When it comes to meeting people:

I am extremely shy. I never know what to say and am very uncomfortable.	I can talk to anybody. Put me in a busy room and I'll know everyone there in no time.

When it comes to self-motivation:

I really need help getting things done. I tend to put everything off until the last moment.	I am extremely self-reliant and never need help getting motivated.

When it comes to change:

I hate change. It makes me so nervous. I need to ease into new situations.	I love to go for it. I like new activities and get bored with routine.

When it comes to doing work:

I am good with details. I get great satisfaction out of taking care of all the details.	I'm a big picture person. I have much more fun figuring out what needs to be done than doing it.

Your Relationship With Money

When you get to Step 2 of this book, you'll look at money in a very practical way—in other words, you'll find out whether you'll have enough of it. But before you get there, take a little time to explore your feelings about money. Thinking about your relationship with money—and your emotional responses to financial challenges—can help you realistically estimate how much money you want from your business and how much you're willing to put in. Consider your feelings about the following issues:

- **Risking your money.** Going out on your own is risky. You could fail. The U.S. Small Business Administration has found that 25% of new businesses disappear within two years of opening, while 50% don't make it past four years. Of course, not all businesses close because of financial trouble; some fold because the owner moves, dies, or decides to do something else. Still, to open a business you have to be willing to take some financial risks.
- **Dipping into your savings.** Cash flow in small businesses tends to be irregular or cyclical. Even when supplemented by monthly income from retirement funds or Social Security, earnings from your retirement business might fall short of your needs, and you may be forced to crack into your retirement nest egg. How will you feel about that? Many retirees are so accustomed to saving that they are very uncomfortable spending those hard-earned dollars.
- **Earnings as a measure of worth.** Your retirement business might prove to be highly profitable. You could match or do better than what you've pulled in for years. But what if you don't? You might find yourself staring at your monthly profit and loss statement, saying, "Why am I knocking myself out, spending so much time on this business? I'm making way less money per hour now than I used to make in my job. I ought to just quit this business and go back to work." If you feel that earnings are a measurement of your value in the workplace, or if making money is your primary motivation for opening a business, a drop in your earnings may be very difficult to swallow.

- **Spending to earn.** Your retirement business will probably require some spending before you earn a single dime. You will have to spend to earn. That's much different than working for someone else, in which case you do your job and earn to spend. It can be nerve-wracking to write a check to the printer for five hundred brochures before you've received any cash from customers. Are you prepared to invest in your business before you see a profit?
- **Over- or under-spending on your business.** Unfortunately, some business owners doom their business from the beginning by incurring too much debt or spending their investment too fast. This can be very tricky if you are accustomed to doing everything first class. But it is also possible to spend too little and starve your business of the resources needed to get the job done. If you tend to pinch every penny, you might have a hard time spending enough to efficiently and profitably serve your customers.
- **Spending habits.** Retirement can lead to changes in your spending habits. When 40 or more hours each week are devoured by work, who has time to shop? In retirement, you might have more time on your hands and find money slipping through your fingers faster than ever. If necessary, can you change your lifestyle and spending habits to match your income? Those who have lived on a shoestring for years, counting pennies and cutting out coupons, might have an emotional advantage when it comes to dealing with cutbacks in retirement. If you've never had to budget household expenditures or account for every penny, having to do so in retirement can be very challenging.

Here's a Tool similar to the previous one, this time with continuums about your relationship with money. You can do this like you did the last Tool, alone or with others.

YOU AND YOUR MONEY

When it comes to risking my money:

I am very risk averse. It makes me shudder to think of losing even a dime in my business.	I have no problem risking my money. Easy come, easy go.

When it comes to money and how I judge my worth:

I don't think money says anything about my value in the workplace. It's not at all that important to me.	How much I earn is the absolute best measure of my value in the work world. It's very important to me.

When it comes to using my retirement nest egg:

I have always been a saver and I definitely would hate to spend down the balance in my retirement accounts.	I have no problem using my retirement money. That's what I saved if for.

When it comes to spending:

I pinch every penny. I'm likely to start my business on a shoestring.	I love to spend and I have very expensive tastes. I will spend as much as necessary to get everything just the way I want it.

MY PROFILE

Completing Your Profile. Before you turn to the next chapter, go to your Profile and fill out the sections that summarize your values, work style, and attitude toward money. When selecting and organizing your new business, you'll appreciate having this handy list of what's most important to you.

Where Will You Live?

He is happiest, be he king or peasant, who finds peace in his home.
—JOHANN VON GOETHE

Maybe you'd like a bigger house—or a smaller one. Maybe you're drawn to winters in a sunny climate, or want to move closer to your daughter and her family in Texas, or can't imagine ever leaving your family home. Deciding where to live is not only important to you personally; it could affect your retirement business opportunity as well.

Some folks have no quandary. They know exactly where they want to be. For others, it's not so easy. Many retirees make several moves in their search for the right location, the right house. Although there's nothing wrong with experimenting or changing your mind, you do need to think about how your choices might affect your new business. Your location may increase or limit your self-employment opportunities.

Where to live can be an especially tricky question for couples. There are two sets of desires and dreams, and it can be a challenge to satisfy both. In addition to helping you decide where you want to spend your retirement years, the Tools in this chapter can stimulate discussion between you and your spouse or partner and help you reach a compromise if you have differing thoughts about where to live.

Location and Your Retirement Business

If you plan to move, the impact on your business future can be significant. You might leave behind your business contacts—those most likely to utilize your services or refer clients. Also, it takes time to learn about a new community and identify what businesses it needs, find the most trustworthy suppliers, or find the best store location. On the bright side, you might be moving to an area with a thriving business environment, full of can-do entrepreneurs and surprising opportunities.

If you don't plan to move, you might find that the business you'd just love to open won't work well where you live. Maybe you've found a franchise you really like—Cold Stone Creamery, perhaps, or U Build It—

but someone already owns the rights to that franchise where you live. In order to take advantage of the opportunity you're excited about, you'd have to open the business in another city. You'd either have to move, hire a manager, or spend most of each week away from home. Don't want to do that? That's okay. Just recognize that your decision not to move may define your opportunities.

Randy loved music. He would travel 90 miles to the nearest big city to immerse himself in rock, jazz, and blues. He wanted to own a nightclub, but couldn't see himself living day-to-day in a city, so he stayed in his blue-collar town. Then, one day, opportunity seemed to knock. The old, dilapidated theater downtown came on the market. It needed lots of work, but would make a terrific music hall. Randy dove into the project, investing much of the money he had saved from his successful management career. He thought he had the business skills, vision, and enthusiasm to make the business work. But it didn't. One year later, Randy closed the business. There simply were not enough music lovers in his small town or neighboring towns to fill his nightclub and bring in a profit. Randy's dream business didn't work in his chosen place to live.

Of course, location might have little or no effect on your business. If you don't mind a little traveling, you can hop a plane in Arizona for a consulting gig in South Dakota, or drive from Denver to Kansas City to visit that all-important supplier. And in today's electronic world, you can run e-commerce businesses from anywhere.

Where's Everybody Going?

Maybe it seems like everyone you know is pulling up stakes and fleeing to a sunny climate, but research indicates that people aged 60 and over are not likely to move far.

The Del Webb Corporation is a leading developer of active adult communities, beginning with Sun City in Arizona. Because their major focus is adults 55 years and older, the corporation spends considerable money and effort on market research about this group. Their 2005 Baby Boomer Annual Opinion Survey showed that older respondents were less likely to move. Of those aged 60–69, only 33% said they planned to buy a new home for retirement, compared to 48% of those aged 50–59.

But if retirees move, where do they go? Yep, you guessed it. Florida and Arizona top the list. Census data shows that from 1995–2000, more people aged 65 and older moved to Florida than any other state, although the percentage of new retirees moving in was lower than in Nevada and Arizona.

The sunny states top the list for migrating retirees, but to concentrate solely on these states would be to ignore a large number of people. For example, Colorado, Washington, Nevada, and Virginia have all seen many retirees crossing their borders and are likely to see more. That is because warm, sunny weather is not the only criterion retirees use in deciding where to live. A recent AARP survey added the following factors to the list:

- availability of jobs
- affordable housing
- culture and entertainment
- access to outdoor recreation
- safety—personal and property
- colleges or universities nearby
- sense of community
- well-regarded health care facilities
- good public high schools, and
- ease of getting around.

Your own list may include many additional factors. At the end of this chapter, we'll help you evaluate a comprehensive list of criteria so you can determine where you can make your happiest life in retirement.

More Information From AARP

AARP Magazine's website is a great place to find information about places to live in retirement. It regularly profiles up-and-coming cities for retirees—for instance, a recent article praised the following "dream towns":

- Las Cruces, New Mexico
- Charleston, South Carolina
- Rehoboth Beach, Delaware
- Memphis, Tennessee
- St. George, Utah

Even better, AARP offers a "Location Scout" that you can use to identify potential locations by giving your own answers to questions about climate, taxes, health, and so on. Go to www.aarpmagazine.org for more—and, if you think you want to move, check out the additional Tools and resources at the end of this chapter.

Snowbirds and Sunbirds

Summers up north. Winters in the south. Sound like the good life? It certainly does to the estimated one million snowbirds who flock to Florida each winter, and to the hundreds of thousands of snowbirds contributing more than $1 billion to Arizona's economy, and to the folks who've chosen a nomadic life, traveling from place to place in their RVs.

You might have lost your patience with long, cold winters, shoveling snow or dodging rainstorms. After all, magazine ads show laughing retirees dancing the night away, riding horses into the sunset, and sinking every putt.

Snowbirding could be the perfect retirement lifestyle for you. However, if you are planning to start a business after retiring, you have to consider whether your business can be effectively operated regardless of your physical location. You will have to ensure that you maintain connections with your customers and have access to your materials and suppliers. In this age of information technology, many businesses do allow mobility, and that's the type of business you'll need if you plan to snowbird.

Another possibility for snowbirders is to have a seasonal retirement business. You could make silver jewelry during winters in Florida and sell it at summer festivals in Illinois.

Although arguably fewer than the large number of migrating snowbirds, many residents of hot summer climates head for beach homes or mountain retreats. Choosing a business that accommodates two locations is just as important for sunbirds as it is for snowbirds.

Should You Move?

The happiest moments of my life have been the few which I have passed at home in the bosom of my family.

—THOMAS JEFFERSON

If you think you might want to move, the following Tools are for you. They will help you examine your motives for taking off or staying put. And if you decide you want to go, they'll help you pick the right place.

SKIP AHEAD

I'm not going anywhere. If you won't be moving, you can skip right to your Profile at the end of the chapter, then move on to Step 2 of this book.

If your decision to move or stay involves another person, you may wish to complete these Tools separately (to make more copies, you can use a photocopier or print multiple copies from the CD-ROM) then compare results.

MOVE OR STAY?

For each of the following statements, indicate your agreement using the scale below.

1 = not a concern for me

2 = somewhat of a concern, but not overwhelming

3 = yes, this is something I care about or is true for me

4 = this is very important to me

I have a very comfortable home now and don't think I could find a better one.

All the people I know live here. How could I leave them?

My children are scattered all across the country, so what does it matter where I live?

This house is paid for or will be soon. Why would I move now and take on new debt?

I've got my shop/sewing room/den/garden exactly how I want it.

I get very good medical care here and I don't want to have to find a new doctor.

Almost all of our friends have moved. This community just isn't the same.

I just can't see myself being far from my children and grandchildren, who all live close by.

I lived in this place because of my job. Now I am free to try a new place.

I am still young and healthy. I want to go while I can.

All of my friends have moved to the same sunny community and I want to join them.

I always wanted to get out of the city and this is my chance.

I've been going to the same hairdresser/grocer/mechanic for all these years. It sounds like too much of a risk and too much trouble to change.

This city/state is far too expensive. I want to move someplace cheaper.

MOVE OR STAY?, continued

I remember the town where I grew up. It was a wonderful place and I want to go back.

This house is worth a bundle. I could sell it and buy a house somewhere else for much less money. I could use the excess sales proceeds to fund my retirement.

My children have moved to another state/city and I want to move closer to them.

I feel stuck in a rut. I'm ready for a change.

My home is my legacy to my children, so I want to keep it.

I want to be close to my favorite activity (fishing/sporting events/ opera/drag racing), so that means I'll have to move.

I've always dreamed of living on a houseboat/in a log cabin/in the mountains/at the beach. That means I'll have to move.

Starting a retirement business is very important to me and I want to live where there is the most potential for success, so I am willing to move.

Your responses to the Tool above should help bring issues to the forefront. Did you notice any passionate responses? Any "1" or "4" answers? These responses can help focus your attention on what is really important to you. The end result of your deliberations should be a decision about whether to move or not.

If you would not be moving alone, hopefully you and your spouse or partner reacted similarly to the statements. If not, openly discuss areas of agreement and disagreement and try to reach a compromise.

If you decide to pull up stakes, you can use the next Tool to choose criteria for where you'd like to go. Before you start, you might find it useful to look back at the interests you identified in Chapter 1; these can have a big effect on where you want to live.

This is another good Tool to do separately from your spouse or partner, then compare results.

FACTORS TO CONSIDER WHEN YOU MOVE

Review the list below to identify the factors that are most important to you, or invent your own. Write your criteria on the ten lines below, but do not rank them. Scramble them instead. For example, put the first factor you think of in blank 10, the second in 3—get the picture? Mixing things up is important for the next Tool.

1. ______________________
2. ______________________
3. ______________________
4. ______________________
5. ______________________
6. ______________________
7. ______________________
8. ______________________
9. ______________________
10. ______________________

Close to family or friends
Easy access to an airport
Lots of fishing/hiking/hunting
Lower income/sales/property taxes
A very secure community
Near a university
Fresh air with little pollution
Political climate matching my opinions
Good public transportation
Good market for my business
Not too far from a city
High property value appreciation
In a foreign country
Great variety of good restaurants
Great local sports teams
Near to other retirees
Small-town atmosphere
Uncrowded
Good medical care

Warm, sunny climate
A good church community available
A climate with four distinct seasons
Access to shopping
Many cultural activities available
Many golf courses close by
Easy to get around, no traffic jams
Many adult education possibilities
Near the mountains/beach/desert
Low cost of living
Low crime rate
Affordable housing
Good Internet access
Lots of routes for daily walks
A mixed-age neighborhood
Temperatures never too hot
Multicultural
In the Northeast/Southeast/Midwest/West/Northwest/Southwest

In this final Tool, you will rank the ten factors you just identified. If you are doing these exercises with a spouse or partner, first agree on which factors to use. This may take some compromise. Be sure to list your factors without considering priorities. If necessary, you may include more than ten factors, but it is possible to get too many to comfortably evaluate.

YOUR KEY FACTORS

Step 1: Start with your list of factors above. Compare two at a time, using the chart below. Compare #1 to #2. Circle the one more important to you. Then, compare #2 to #3. Which is more important? Continue comparing your criteria, moving across the rows, until all have been compared.

1 2	2 3	3 4	4 5	5 6	6 7	7 8	8 9	9 10
1 3	2 4	3 5	4 6	5 7	6 8	7 9	8 10	
1 4	2 5	3 6	4 7	5 8	6 9	7 10		
1 5	2 6	3 7	4 8	5 9	6 10			
1 6	2 7	3 8	4 9	5 10				
1 7	2 8	3 9	4 10					
1 8	2 9	3 10						
1 9	2 10							
1 10								

Step 2: Count the number of times each factor was circled. The more times you circled a factor, the higher its priority. Now, rewrite your list of factors from most to least important. If you are working with a partner, compare and discuss your results when you finish.

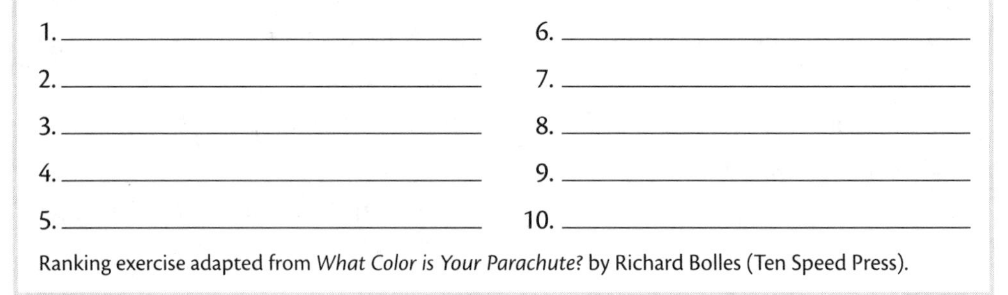

1. ______________________ 6. ______________________
2. ______________________ 7. ______________________
3. ______________________ 8. ______________________
4. ______________________ 9. ______________________
5. ______________________ 10. ______________________

Ranking exercise adapted from *What Color is Your Parachute?* by Richard Bolles (Ten Speed Press).

Researching Places to Live

Happiness is having a large, loving, caring, close-knit family in another city.
—GEORGE BURNS

Once you've identified the most important factors for where you'd like to live, the next step is finding the cities or towns that best match your wishes. The most common research method is talking to people. If the Gerbers just bought in Yuma, Arizona, you can quiz them about how they made their choice. You might learn that they checked out Yuma by talking with the Smiths, who moved there after talking to the Johnsons. Word-of-mouth is a great research technique, especially if you can do it first-hand rather than relying on someone else's interpretation of what the Johnsons really said about Yuma. Who better to give you the real scoop about living somewhere than people who live there?

However, be sure to use your criteria for selecting a location, not theirs. The Johnsons may rave about the cheap golf in Yuma. That may have been right at the top of their list of essential factors. If it's not at the top of yours, be sure to ask about what does matter to you. Use your Tools to get a firm grasp on your personal criteria about where to live. Keep your list handy and refer to it when you interview others.

It's also important to talk to retirees. You can get good information by talking to your nephew who lives in Charleston, but if he has three young children at home and his biggest worries are losing his job and rush-hour traffic, he may not be able to give you good information about what matters most to you.

The Internet is another way to research places to live. You can use websites to find articles, personal stories, studies, and economic data. We've listed some of our favorite resources at the end of this chapter.

Finally, talking to people and visiting websites can help you refine your choices, but there's no better research than actually being there. At minimum, you could visit cities you are considering, but just a visit might not give you insight into daily life there. If possible, spend a month in the place or places you are considering. Rent an apartment or a house. Compare your experience to your where-to-move criteria.

Of course, testing the waters is not for everyone. You may be set on selling your house and moving right away, with no time or energy for dilly-dallying or long decision-making processes. You'll make a choice and if it turns out wrong, you'll just pull up stakes and move again. Other than the hard work that moving always seems to involve, there's nothing wrong with this approach, but you will have to choose your retirement business carefully. Make sure it is portable. Otherwise, if you don't like where you moved, you'll have to either stay and put up with your location in order to keep the business going, or give up on the business and start over again somewhere else.

RESOURCE

Helpful books. The following books can help you gather information about places to live:

America's 100 Best Places to Retire: The Only Guide You Need to Today's Top Retirement Towns, by Elizabeth Armstrong (Vacation Publications), contains lots of statistics about retirement towns as well as interviews with people who have relocated to each town.

Retirement Places Rated: What You Need to Know to Plan the Retirement You Deserve, by David Savageau (Frommers), ranks 200 places to live in retirement based on detailed statistical profiles.

Cities Ranked and Rated: More Than 400 Metropolitan Areas Evaluated in the U.S. and Canada, by Peter Sander (Wiley), is not aimed at retirees but it covers over 400 metropolitan areas in the United States and Canada.

Help on the Web

In addition to the AARP website mentioned earlier (www.aarpmagazine.org), you can get help from the following Internet sites:

- **www.bestplaces.net.** You can compare cost of living, crime rates, climate, and other factors at Sperling's Best Places website. As with AARP's Location Scout, this site will quiz you about various criteria and respond with a list of suggested cities. Some information is available free of charge or you can purchase a membership.
- **www.findyourspot.com.** This site offers yet another location quiz—presented with much humor. You can include small and midsized towns in your results.
- **www.bankrate.com/brm/movecalc.asp.** Bankrate.com doesn't charge you a penny to compare the cost of living in various cities.
- **www.CNNmoney.com.** CNN Money, the Internet site for *Fortune, Money*, and other magazines, conducts annual studies and selects the Best Places to Live. You can see their 2006 selections at http://money.cnn.com/magazines/moneymag/bplive/2006/index.html.
- **www.cityrating.com.** This handy website offers profiles and statistics for hundreds of cities.

MY PROFILE

Completing Your Profile. You know what to do next. Go to your Profile and complete the "Location" section. You'll want all of this information in one place when it's time to evaluate business ideas.

Inventory Your Resources

You won't go into your new business empty handed. You've got three possible resources to help you: skills, time, and money. Taking stock of your resources lets you know right up front what you have to work with and what you'll need to add. You can use your inventory to help find your best business idea and check to see if it's really feasible.

This step helps you answer these important questions:

- What are your skills?
- How will you spend your time?
- Will you have enough money?

Chapter 4 will help you inventory your skills, any one of which might lead to a business idea. When thinking about your skills, you'll consider all of your life experiences, not just what you've learned at work. In **Chapter 5**, you'll envision how you want to spend your time in retirement, including the hours you'll devote to your business. Finally, the last part of this step—**Chapter 6**—is all about money. You'll complete a series of easy-to-understand Tools to get a realistic picture of your finances. This will help you determine two things: how much you have available to start your business, and how much income you want to get out of it.

As you did in the last step, you'll summarize your resource inventory in your Retirement Business Profile, and you'll be well on your way to selecting your number one business idea.

CHAPTER

What Are Your Skills?

Use what talent you possess: The woods would be very silent if no birds sang except those that sang best.
—HENRY VAN DYKE

This chapter helps you take stock of the wide range of skills you have developed over the years. There are two ways you can use your skills to help you decide what kind of business to start in retirement:

- You can use a list of your skills to look for business ideas that match what you've got to offer, and
- You can consult your skills list when you check the feasibility of your chosen business idea.

You'll get to both of these tasks a little later in the book; first, you've got to take inventory of your many abilities.

When you think of your skills, you probably focus on those you have developed and used at various jobs. This is a natural tendency and, of course, work skills are very important. However, most people also develop skills in other ways: attending school, raising a family, engaging in recreational activities, volunteering. So, keep a broad perspective when thinking about your skills.

To give you a general idea of the skills you'll need to run your retirement business, we begin by discussing the two roles that you must fill: worker and owner. Then, we give you Tools to take stock of your own skills, which you'll summarize in your Profile and use to help find the right retirement business for you.

Two Roles: Worker and Owner

In large organizations, there are many roles and people tend to specialize. There are managers, supervisors, technical experts, support staff, line workers, and so on. Seldom does a manager unload trucks or weld metal components. And seldom does a welder negotiate a sales contract or prepare a staffing schedule.

The same tasks may need to be done in a small business, but now there are fewer people to do them. In fact, you might be the only one. When you are self-employed, you have no choice but to assume two roles—the worker and the owner. If you pay too little attention to either role, your business will suffer and most likely fail.

In your role as worker, you will perform the everyday tasks in the business. You'll be the chef or the salesclerk, the tax return preparer or the mechanic. As a worker, you will use your technical skills to serve customers. If you're good at what you do, your customers will pay for those skills.

But customers will find your business—and return to it—because of your skills as an owner. In your owner role, you will provide the vision, strategies, and methods to make your business successful. It will be your job to keep things running smoothly—ensuring that all critical tasks happen on time, within budget, and at a level of quality that meets your standards. And you'll have clerical tasks to handle—keeping records, filing taxes, and making sure that your business complies with government regulations. When you are a business owner, it is always true that "the buck stops here."

Sally worked for the statewide restaurant association for 25 years. During her last 12 years she managed the annual trade show, industry seminars, and numerous promotional events for the association. She supervised a staff of four and worked with many committees of restaurant owners to make the events successful.

After retiring from the restaurant association, Sally started a consulting business. She uses her managerial skills to help other industry associations organize their annual trade shows.

Skills for either one of these roles might lead you to a business idea. Most people who become self-employed choose a business in which they have, or can obtain, the skills to do the work. You might be eager to start a business that features your ability to tune up cars, counsel families, prepare food, write software, or build houses.

But you also could open a business that primarily uses your owner skills and hire others to be the workers. Just because you aren't an expert welder doesn't mean you can't own a welding shop, although it would help to know at least something about it. If your owner skills are strong, you can manage almost any kind of business.

Or, you could turn your owner skills (like managing, or strategic planning, or organizing, or marketing) into what you offer customers.

You probably have more skills to bring to your roles as worker and owner than you realize. Coming up, you'll find two Tools to help you list the skills you are aware of and identify those you may not have considered.

Joe retired after working for 28 years as an auto mechanic for the local Ford dealer. He liked the work, but a back injury made it impossible to continue. His initial list of worker skills focused on tune-ups, brake jobs, replacing transmissions, and the many other tasks he had routinely performed. When he started thinking beyond his job, however, his list grew:

Joe owned several rental properties. He remodeled and maintained these properties himself. So he listed his construction skills.

He had coached soccer when his children were playing and then became the coordinator of the annual local soccer fundraiser for the last six years. Joe listed his coaching and fundraising skills.

Joe was also an amateur photographer. He cut the mats and made the frames for his photos. So he listed all of these skills.

Once his list of worker skills was complete Joe felt optimistic about finding a business opportunity outside of being a mechanic.

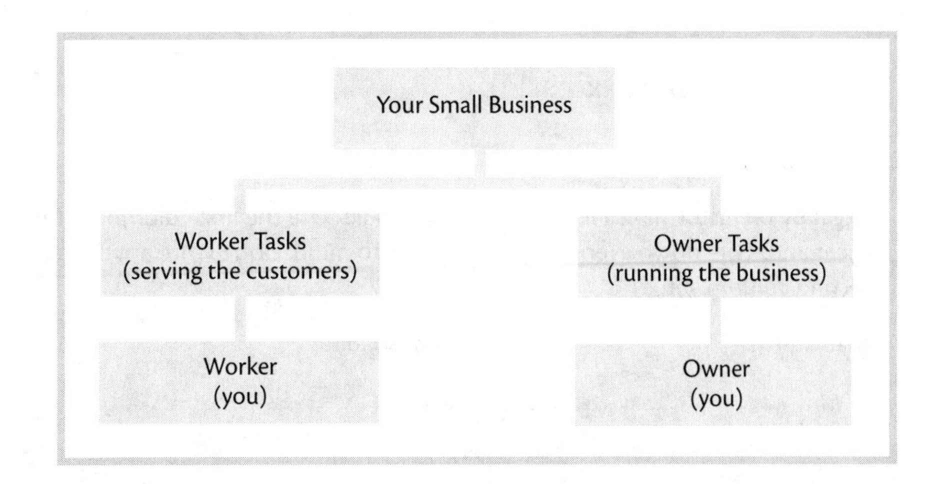

Worker Skills

Do what you can, with what you have, where you are.

—THEODORE ROOSEVELT

In the following Tool, you will identify worker skills you have developed during your life and that you enjoy using. Remember, your worker skills may come from work, school, volunteering, hobbies, running a home, raising kids, or other activities. (You might jog your thinking by looking back at the Tools in Chapter 1 where you listed your interests.) And they may come from your life experiences at any age. It is important to identify all of your skills; for now, don't make judgments about the feasibility of basing a business on a particular skill. A broad list will help you think about a wider range of possible business opportunities, and make self-employment more exciting.

We realize it can sometimes be difficult to distinguish a worker skill from an owner skill. For example, if your career has been as a purchasing agent, then you might say that negotiating prices and scheduling deliveries are some of your worker skills. These skills also might be needed in your role as business owner. Don't worry about which category to use; just be sure to include all of your skills in one of the next Tools.

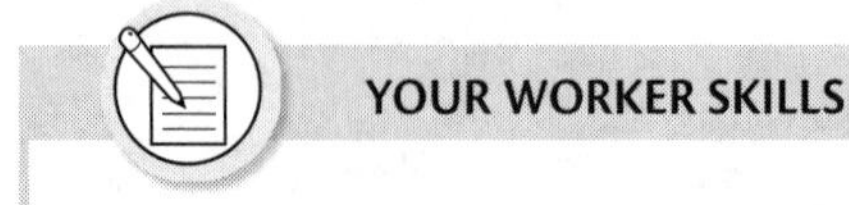

YOUR WORKER SKILLS

Step 1: Brainstorm!

Begin by brainstorming a list of your worker skills. Use the first column of the worksheet and write down everything that comes to mind. Don't write anything in the second column yet.

Brainstorm	Consolidate

Step 2: Eliminate skills that you don't enjoy.

Review your list and cross out any skills you don't enjoy using or that don't give you satisfaction.

Step 3: Eliminate the unproven.

Now eliminate any skills you haven't actually demonstrated. This is not a list of skills you wish you had. Stick to proven abilities. You can consider skills you plan to acquire in a later chapter when you search for business ideas.

Step 4: Consolidate and clarify.

You probably listed some of your skills several times by using different words. Take a few minutes to combine similar skills into groups. Use the second column of the worksheet. This is also a chance to add new skills to your list.

Step 5: Prioritize.

What skills will you use in your business? Circle the abilities that you'd most like to put to work.

Owner Skills

There are certain types of owner skills common to owners of all businesses. As mentioned above, all owners must keep records, pay taxes, and follow the laws. All owners must handle the marketing and management of their business. But some owner skills may be important in one type of business and not in others. For example, managing inventory is important if you will be selling lots of different products but it is not a critical skill if you have a service business. The ability to supervise employees can be important, but if you'll be a one-person business, it doesn't matter. Nevertheless, the best place to start is by making a comprehensive list of your owner skills—and the following Tool will guide you.

As with worker skills, your owner skills may come from a wide array of experiences, from work and volunteering to traveling or raising pets. Don't judge the feasibility of managing a business using a specific skill; for now, just add it to your list.

Owner Skills

When listing your skills, it may help to think of common business functions such as the following:

- **Planning:** defining mission and vision, setting goals, writing business plans, budgeting
- **Marketing and Sales:** choosing target markets, selecting pricing strategies, developing promotional plans
- **Finance and Accounting:** analyzing expenses, obtaining financing, identifying profitable segments of a business
- **Operations:** purchasing, scheduling production, controlling inventory, developing new products and services
- **Supervision:** hiring and firing, reviewing performance, assigning workloads, training.

YOUR OWNER SKILLS

Step 1: Brainstorm!

It's time to brainstorm another list. This time, list your owner skills. Use the first column in the worksheet and write down all the owner skills you can think of. Save the second column for later.

Brainstorm	Consolidate

Step 2: Eliminate skills that you don't enjoy.

Review your list and cross out any skills you don't enjoy using or that don't give you satisfaction.

Step 3: Eliminate the unproven.

Now eliminate any skills that you have not yet demonstrated. This is not a list of skills you wish you had or plan to develop, but rather actual skills.

Step 4: Consolidate and clarify.

You probably listed some skills several times by using different words. Use the second column and spend a few minutes combining similar skills into groups. You also can use this step as a chance to add new skills to your list.

Step 5: Prioritize.

Circle the owner skills that you would like to use in your retirement business.

CD-EXTRA!

Fill your skills gaps. It's not likely that you're good at all of the owner tasks that your business will require. And, even if you are skilled at a task, you might not enjoy doing it. Once you've chosen your business idea, check out the Extras! file on the CD-ROM for a Tool to help you identify gaps in your skills inventory and plan how you'll fill those gaps.

MY PROFILE

Completing Your Profile. Before you turn the page, go to your Profile and complete the section about skills. The Profile will help you summarize your skills so you can use them to look for business ideas and zero in on the balance of worker and owner skills that you wish to achieve in your new business.

CHAPTER

How Will You Spend Your Time?

You will never "find" time for anything. If you want time you must make it.
—CHARLES BUXTON

You, like most people, probably haven't developed a plan for how you will spend your time in retirement. "But wait!" you may say. Isn't retirement supposed to be about not having to organize your time?

Not if you want to start your own business.

A new business can easily require every hour you are willing to give it—and more. And what about all those other activities you'd like to pursue: going to concerts, learning to kayak, volunteering at the wildlife rescue center? You'll feel better about your new life if you make a plan that balances work and play.

The Tools in this chapter will help you envision how you'll spend your time during retirement. The main goal is to determine how much time you can devote to your retirement business, but you will also give plenty of attention to the other things you want and need to do.

One way to go about this would be to think just about the hours you've spent working and how you'll spend them in retirement. What will you do with the 40 hours per week spent at your job and the ten hours commuting? However, thinking only about these hours makes the assumption that the rest of your life won't change—and that's not normally the case. You're also likely to find changes in the time you spend doing household chores, caring for others, traveling, and playing.

That's why we take a different approach to thinking about time. We ask you to consider all of your hours and activities, estimate how much time you'll spend on them, and see how it all adds up. You might find that you've got hours to spare or, like many of us, you'll see that you've planned to use more hours in a day than you've got. Our method helps you envision the whole of your life, building in time for running your business so you can see where it fits into the big picture.

Finding Time for a Business

Where will you find the time to devote to your retirement business? It might come from reducing time spent in one or more of three main roles.

According to John Robinson and Geoffrey Godbey, authors of *Time for Life*, there are three factors that greatly influence how you spend your time and the amount of free time you have:

- employment
- marriage, and
- parenting.

When you reduce your time commitment to one of these roles—at retirement, for example—you suddenly have significant amounts of free time. This is magnified for many people as they reduce time spent in two of the three roles almost at once. It is common to end parenting duties and then retire within a few years. That can be exciting, but it also can cause anxiety for some people about how they'll fill all those hours. But lucky you—the extra time is just what you'll need to get your business going.

How Will You Spend a Typical Year?

Life is what happens while you're making other plans.
—JOHN LENNON

The amount of time you are willing and able to commit to owning a business is a major factor in choosing an appropriate business opportunity. Some businesses can be successful in just a few hours per day, while others require the same time commitment as a full-time job. To figure out how much time you can give, you'll first take a look at how you'd like to divide your time during a typical year—that is, how many weeks you'll devote to work, travel, and other pursuits. Then, in coming sections, you'll consider how you want to spend your hours in a typical week. At the end, you'll use your profile to complete a summary that will help you choose the business that's best for you.

A Dose of Reality

As you think about your time in retirement, try to be as realistic as possible. Most retirees say that they spend more time on everyday tasks than before. They read the newspaper cover to cover, clean the house more often, spend more time with grandchildren. You may also spend more time taking care of your own health or helping others who rely on you. You'll consider shifts like these as you complete the Tools in this chapter; the exercises are designed, in part, to help you anticipate such changes.

For the following brief Tool, envision how many weeks you want to spend working, traveling, and taking care of things at home after you have started your retirement business. Count weeks spent on your business as weeks spent working. If you also plan to take a job, count those as working weeks, too. Remember that your total should be 52 weeks.

YOUR TYPICAL YEAR

	During Retirement
Weeks Spent Working	
Weeks Spent Traveling	
Weeks at Home, Not Working	

How Much Time Will You Spend Working?

Work is usually the number one use of our waking hours. A typical work week is defined as 40 hours, but the average American male works 49 hours per week while women average 42 hours. And these figures reflect only paid, working hours spent at a primary job. Many Americans work at least two jobs or are also self-employed to earn extra money.

When you retire, you may reduce the total number of hours you work in two ways. First, you may work fewer weeks per year. Second, you may work fewer hours in a typical week. This could net you quite a lot of free time.

Dave recently retired from his primary job as a city building inspector. He decided to devote 20 hours per week to his home-based business of reviewing building plans for people hiring a general contractor. He also plans to take eight weeks of vacation instead of the three weeks he has taken in recent years. Dave will be working five fewer weeks and 27 hours less during his typical work week. He has gained over 1,000 hours of time!

The next Tool addresses your work week—the time you'd like to devote to work in retirement. Assume for the moment that you have identified a business that is right for you. Include the number of hours you wish to work per week and any related time, such as time for breaks and meals. Consider, too, any time required for your daily commute. Hours you work with no expectation of being paid, such as volunteering, will be addressed in other Tools.

This Tool focuses on how many hours you want to devote to your new venture. A later Tool will help you figure out whether your number of hours is realistic.

YOUR WORK TIME

	Hours Per Week During Retirement
Working on Your Retirement Business	
Working at a Job	
Other:	
Weeks at Home, Not Working	
Total Work Hours Per Week	

What About Time for Yourself?

The important thing is not to stop questioning.
—ALBERT EINSTEIN

How will you approach using your free time in retirement? Let yourself muse about what you'd like to do:

- What new skills would you like to acquire?
- Do you want to take classes to learn new things?
- Do you look forward to reading for pleasure?
- Is travel the way you discover the world?
- Will sporting events play an important role in your life?
- Do you plan to attend local live performances?
- Is it time to visit the many museums you never had time to see?
- How about music in local nightclubs now that you can get up later in the morning?

This section focuses on several important categories you might like to explore: keeping your brain in shape, taking care of your health, volunteering your time, and pure play—entertainment and recreation. Many of these activities relate to the goals you identified in Chapter 1; so, before you start this section, take a look at the work you did there. If a goal is truly SMARTPLUS, you'll build time for it into the Tools below.

We realize that some of the categories can be difficult to distinguish. If you volunteer to help decorate the church you attend, should you list those hours as volunteering or as spiritual growth? Don't worry too much about that. Our categories are meant to jog your thinking. The important thing is to consider all uses of your time and estimate those hours somewhere, without duplication.

Exercising your mind. It is important to keep your mind active during retirement. Your retirement business will keep your brain cells working but you'll want to consider other forms of mental exercise as well.

Retirement can be a great time to learn more about the many things you have found interesting during your life, or to discover brand new things. You might read, watch documentaries, or attend lectures in your community. You could join a local book club, visit historical sites, or stretch your mind in countless other ways. If you like more structure, you can check out the offerings at your local community college or explore the lifelong learning catalogue from a nearby university.

Dino, a long-haul trucker, and **Elle,** a legal secretary, have been competent and dependable workers, but their jobs have rarely provided exciting challenges or opportunities to learn new skills. They view their work as just the daily repetition of rather mundane tasks. In retirement, they're excited by the idea of learning new subjects and discovering new facets of life. Dino wants to accomplish his learning by taking adult education classes at night and reading. Elle is looking forward to self-study classes at home and lectures at the local university. They will also take a two-week trip to a new location every year.

Helping out. Many organizations make valuable contributions to the community. These organizations are always looking for volunteers or members. If you haven't had time to be a volunteer, you may want to begin after you retire. If you've been an active volunteer, you may be looking forward to doing more. On the other hand, if you've put in a life of service, you may never again want to see another committee, fundraiser, or board meeting.

If you want to volunteer your time but aren't sure where to start, check with your local senior center, church, or RSVP (Retired Seniors Volunteer Program) to learn about your options. Some people contribute their time to their professional association as a way of staying in touch with colleagues. Or, you can contact your local Chamber of Commerce for a list of local civic, fraternal, environmental, and political organizations. Many of them will be glad to have a new volunteer.

Steve and Wanda are planning to retire in a few months. Steve has been the branch manager of a bank and has been active in numerous community organizations as part of his job. He has had enough meetings to last a lifetime and heard every possible local speaker. When he retires, he has vowed that he will be involved in only one organization. But Wanda has been a bookkeeper in a medical office and raised three children, leaving her little chance to be active in the community. She wants to become an active volunteer. Wanda is ready to give back to the community that has been her home for so many years.

Entertainment. You could spend many hours listening to music, going to plays, watching movies, visiting art galleries, or cheering at sporting events. You may continue to do the things you've always done or discover new forms of entertainment.

Your retirement business may give you the flexibility to attend events that occur on weekdays or take place late at night. There are options in your community that you probably didn't notice when you were working.

Recreation. Recreation is a broad category and some activities overlap with entertainment. For our purposes, recreation means actively participating in something, such as a golf league, softball team, biking group, or tennis club. Less physical activities such as playing cards and games, scanning your old photos onto your computer, and crocheting also count as recreation.

Taking care of yourself. Bathing, shaving, eating, going to the doctor—personal care takes a great number of hours each week. As you age, you can expect to spend more time taking care of your health, from doctor and dentist appointments to daily medications and other therapies. Even if health problems don't crop up right away, you may choose to make good health a focus of your new life—for example, by making more time for exercise and relaxation.

You might also include in this category hours you plan to spend on personal growth through religion or spiritual practices.

Sleeping. This activity needs no explanation but it does deserve its own category. This may be your greatest use of time. Getting enough sleep will help you enjoy your waking hours.

Larry and Sally moved to Seattle after they retired from their teaching jobs in Montana. They enjoyed working and raising their kids in a small ranching town with a very safe and family-oriented environment. However, after retiring they began to feel bored with small-town life. Their children had moved away to find jobs and many of their friends left after retiring. Larry's self-employment business—reviewing new science textbooks—was easy to relocate anywhere. After lots of research, they decided to move to Seattle. They wanted the mild climate, professional sports, museums, concerts, and theater. Their three years in Seattle have been full of entertainment activities.

Complete this next Tool with the number of hours you expect to spend each week for the above activities. Remember—be as realistic as you can.

TIME FOR YOURSELF

	Hours Per Week During Retirement
Learning	
Volunteering	
Entertainment	
Recreation	
Taking Care of Yourself	
Sleeping	
Total Hours for Yourself Per Week	

What Are Your Personal Obligations?

If you find it in your heart to care for somebody else, you will have succeeded.
—MAYA ANGELOU

In this section, you will consider the number of hours you'll spend taking care of your loved ones and your home.

Taking care of others. Consider those in your life who need your care now. Then reflect on whether it's likely that someone will need you as a caregiver later on. Possibilities may include your grandchildren, your aging parents, or your spouse, if he or she develops health problems that require your attention. And there may be other surprises: Divorced or unemployed children may ask to live with you to reduce expenses, or a good friend with no close family may turn to you for help. Think about your pets, too. As they get older, you may devote many hours to their care.

Of course, you won't be able to know precisely how many hours you'll spend caring for others in the future. If you're married or partnered, talk things over together. Make your best guesses about what might be coming. If you think it's likely that others will need your care, account for it when you complete the Tool below.

Dave and Mary both have jobs that require working 50 to 60 hours per week. Because of their busy schedules, they eat in restaurants almost every weeknight. They also save time by hiring a housekeeper and yard maintenance service. After they retire, Dave and Mary plan to save money by eating at home more often and taking care of their home and yard themselves.

Household chores. Whether you like it or not, shopping, doing laundry, and handling other household chores take a great number of hours each week. And retirement often means that you'll spend even more time at home, with even more chores to do. (This is especially true if your retirement business is home based.) There will be more dirty dishes, more dirt tracked in, more time to notice that the lawn needs mowing again.

Money may make a difference in how you spend your personal time. For example, if you will have less available income after you retire, you may have to spend more time taking care of things that you used to hire others to do.

TIME FOR OBLIGATIONS

	Hours Per Week During Retirement
Taking Care of Others	
Household Chores	
Total Hours for Obligations Per Week	

There Are Only 168 Hours in a Week

Now it's time to take stock of what you've done in the Tools above. This chapter's final Tool summarizes your estimated retirement week. Refer to the previous Tools and complete the column below.

YOUR 168 HOURS

	Hours Per Week During Retirement
Total Hours: Work	
Total Hours: For Yourself	
Total Hours: For Obligations	
Your Total Hours	

Have you accounted for all 168 hours you have per week? Or, have you overdone it, totaling more than 168? If your total wasn't 168 or very close to it, spend some time reviewing and revising your responses to the previous Tools.

Using your time in a way that brings you satisfaction is very important as you plan your retirement. It's especially important that you recognize your time commitments before choosing your retirement business. If you accounted for more than 168 hours, you'll have to reduce something. Will it be time spent on your business? Or, will you play golf three days per week instead of five? Take a look at the hours you estimated for your business and think about whether you could spend more or less. The amount of time you can give will be significant in choosing the right business for you.

TIP

Time Management. People who make time for a wide variety of activities tend to feel less stressed and more satisfied. How can you create the time that you can't seem to find now? Be systematic. These hints may help you:

- **Set goals.** At least once a year, develop a list of goals. This list should include what you want to achieve personally and for your business. Use what you learned in Chapter 1 to set realistic, measurable goals.
- **Keep a "To Do" list.** Maintain a list of tasks that you need to complete. Assign a priority and completion date to each task. Update your list at least once a week. Crossing off tasks will give you a sense of accomplishment.
- **Use a time-planning system.** You can use a paper- or computer-based system. Or go digital and buy a PDA (personal digital assistant) that you can link to your computer. But keep in mind that the technology you choose isn't what will make the system work. You are the key. Use the system to stay organized and gain control over your time.
- **Keep an activity log.** This is a record of how you actually spend your time. You'll probably find it easiest to keep this information in your time-planning system. At the end of each month, review the record of how you are actually spending your time. Are you finishing the high priority tasks that help you accomplish your goals? Congratulations if you are. If not, it's time to reconsider your priorities.

MY PROFILE

Completing Your Profile. Go to your Retirement Business Profile and fill in the brief section that summarizes your preferences and needs regarding time for your business. Your Profile is nearly finished. Just one more chapter to go; then you will turn your attention to finding great business ideas and choosing the best one for you.

CHAPTER

6

Will You Have Enough Money?

The safest way to double your money is to fold it over once and put it in your pocket.
—KIN HUBBARD

As you plan for retirement, the subject of money may concern you more than any other. It certainly gets plenty of attention. There are television specials, magazine articles, and quizzes on websites to help you determine whether you are financially ready to retire. Investment companies fill the airwaves with ads about building a nest egg. And money is the most common topic covered in books about retirement. We want you to focus on more than money as you consider your retirement, but understanding your financial situation is a critical factor in choosing the right business for you.

In this chapter, you will take an objective look at your finances. The Tools will help you catalogue each of your investments and evaluate your debts. You'll also find Tools to help you project your monthly income and expenses after retirement. (You may already have a financial plan in place, perhaps one that was prepared by a financial planner or accountant. Refer to it and you should be able to complete these Tools fairly easily.)

By the time you finish this chapter, you will have a summary of your financial situation in hand. You will know how much you feel comfortable investing in your retirement business—and how much you want to earn from it.

Financial Realities and Unknowns

The excitement of trying something new, of opening your retirement business, might be dampened by fear of running out of money. Outliving your financial resources is a scary scenario. You need a sound financial plan to fund your retirement dreams. Making such a plan can put many of your concerns to rest.

Putting together a financial plan involves what you know—for example, the balance in your accounts today—and what you don't know but can predict for the future. When looking ahead, you should keep in mind a number of financial realties and several big unknowns. We'll consider each of them here.

Retiring young. You may have the goal of retiring earlier (and living longer) than your parents. This would mean spending many more years in retirement than they did. You could be retired for more years than you worked! That's a lot of retirement living expenses to be financed and it will require careful planning.

Changing spending habits. Spending less during retirement seems logical, but it's not as easy at it sounds. Your work-related expenses will decrease, but you will have more time available to pursue other interests, and that can cost money. Unless you make big changes in your living situation, maintaining your home may continue to be a significant expense. And most people simply don't want to spend less. You will have to assess your priorities.

Skimpy savings. Most people are not financially prepared to retire. Savings in the United States are very low when compared to other developed countries. Americans tend to focus on short-term financial needs and desires.

Inheritance expectations. Perhaps you are counting on inheriting enough money to fund your retirement. Some people receive substantial inheritances, but most of us will receive almost nothing. How much you will inherit, and when, is very hard to predict.

Uncle Sam. You might hope that the government (through Social Security) will take care of your retirement needs. You will probably receive Social Security payments, but the system was never intended to be your sole source of support. And the Social Security system is in trouble, facing a predicted deficit by 2013. Perhaps Congress will act, but much is uncertain. Most experts believe that the system will be restructured to help those most in need—people who aren't covered by a corporate retirement plan and who have little, if any, savings.

Financial needs of Baby Boomers. Ken Dychtwald, in his book, *Age Power*, discusses how the large population of aging Baby Boomers will face retirement financially:

- About one-third of Boomers will be in good shape. These are the people who earned good salaries, made wise investments, and are likely to inherit money when their parents die. Congratulations if you are part of this group! These lucky people may decide to become self-employed but have no pressure to make money from their business.
- A second third of Boomers will end up working at least five years longer than they expected in order to afford retirement. If you are part of this group, you will want to make an informed decision about starting your own business versus continuing to work for someone else. Choosing a profitable business opportunity is critical.
- The final third of Boomers have household net assets of less than $1,000. It is unclear how this bottom third will ever afford to retire. If you haven't saved anything for retirement, you may be faced with two options: work longer than you had planned or reduce your living expenses—or both. A retirement business can help. If you are in this category, you will need to choose a business that doesn't require a huge start-up investment. (You will determine your start-up costs in Chapter 10.)

Three unknowns. Planning for your future requires you to deal with three great unknowns that are addressed in the next three sections of this chapter:

- How long will you live?
- How much will you earn on your investments?
- How will inflation affect your retirement plans?

How Long Will You Live?

The greatest unknown you face is how many more years you will live. This makes it challenging to evaluate your retirement finances. You probably know a coworker, friend, or family member who died unexpectedly in their 40s or early 50s. On the other hand, we know people who are very active in their 70s and 80s and will probably live to be 90 or 100. This presents a wide range of possibilities to consider as you plan for retirement.

Thinking about how many more years you will live is not something you're likely to enjoy; however, you need to make an educated guess as a first step in your planning. If you greatly outlive your expectations, you risk running out of money. For this reason, many people are very financially conservative when making retirement plans.

Life Expectancy

The Centers for Disease Control and Prevention publishes data about life expectancies. Below are average life expectancies as of 2003 (the most current figures available at the time this book was published). Here's how the table works: Find the age closest to yours in the column on the left, and then add the number for your gender to determine the number of additional years you can expect to live. For example, a 60-year-old male can expect to live another 20.4 years. A 75-year-old female can anticipate another 12.5 years.

Current Age	Male	Female
50 years old	28.5	32.3
55 years old	24.3	27.9
60 years old	20.4	23.7
65 years old	16.8	19.7
70 years old	13.4	15.9
75 years old	10.5	12.5
80 years old	7.9	9.5

You can find the most current information about your life expectancy by visiting the Centers for Disease Control and Prevention website at www.cdc.gov. Enter "life expectancy" into the search box.

Of course your lifestyle—diet, exercise, smoking, drinking, stress, and so on—plays a major role in how long you will live. You should also consider your personal health history and that of family members when thinking about your life expectancy.

How Much Will You Earn on Your Investments?

It's tough to make predictions, especially about the future.

—YOGI BERRA

Another great unknown is how much you will earn from your investments. You need to estimate future rates of return to calculate your retirement earnings, though it's not always easy to do this.

During some years, the stock market offers big returns. At other times, almost everyone loses money. Investments that pay you interest, like bonds and certificates of deposit, are more stable but tend to produce very little when inflation is low. Real estate also has its ups and downs, often performing well when stocks deliver less, and vice versa. A good overall guideline to remember is that riskier investments usually have higher average returns than safer ones.

Are Your Investments Insured?

Checking accounts, savings accounts, money market accounts, and certificates of deposit at financial institutions insured by the FDIC (Federal Deposit Insurance Corporation) are protected up to a maximum of $100,000 per depositor for each institution. For example, you and your spouse could have two separate accounts and one joint account at your favorite bank. The separate accounts would each be insured up to $100,000. The joint account would be insured up to $200,000 since there are two owners. Retirement accounts are insured up to $250,000 per individual. But be aware that not all banks and savings associations are FDIC-insured. Many financial institutions, such as brokerage companies, are not FDIC-insured. When you are considering how much you expect to earn from your investments, take the time to note whether or not your money is insured.

To arrive at a realistic rate of return when you make financial projections, you need to balance optimistic and pessimistic viewpoints. On one hand, if you make conservative estimates and your investments earn more than you project, you will have more money to leave your heirs—or to cover expenses if you live longer than expected. But if you're too generous in your projections and your investments earn less than you hope, your heirs could get less or you could outlive your resources. We recommend a cautious approach. (See "Forecasting Investment Income: Be Conservative," below.)

If you use the services of a financial consultant, ask for advice about rates of return to use when planning for your retirement. Here are some tips to help you make educated estimates of the rates of return you can expect during retirement:

Susan just retired, at age 60, from her marketing research position with a software company. According to the figures from the CDC Susan can expect to live another 23.7 years. Her father just celebrated his 88th birthday and many of her relatives have lived to be at least 85. Susan exercises regularly, eats a well-balanced diet, doesn't smoke or drink, and controls her weight.

Susan is single, not anticipating an inheritance, and plans to work as a consultant and trainer for at least five years. It is very important to her that she not outlive her sources of income. Susan decided to plan her retirement based on living to 93, almost a full ten years longer than the CDC figure.

- **Rate of return and inflation.** A conservative approach to predicting future returns is to say they'll equal annual inflation. If your investments don't earn enough to match increasing costs of living, then you are losing ground. (We discuss inflation in more detail, below.)
- **Current rates of return and the future.** Current rates are better predictors of short-term future returns than long-term. While there's no guarantee that current rates will continue, you should at least be familiar with them. You can use them as a starting point for your predictions.

- **Historical rates of return and the future.** You may want to look at historical long-term returns for your investments, but remember that the past is not necessarily a good indication of the future. Also, the years you consider can make a huge difference in the returns you see. For example, the S&P (Standard & Poor's) 500 stock index gained 91.47% for the ten years 1997 through 2006; however, it gained 54.99% in the first five of those years and only 23.54% in the last five. The difference is even more dramatic for the ten years through 2005: These years show a total return of 102.67%—with 114.36% in the first five years but a loss of 5.45% in the last five. Significant variations also exist between industries, sectors of the economy, and regions of the world.

Rates of Return

Type of Asset or Investment Product	Rate of Return
Cash. Some people keep substantial amounts of cash in a house safe, in a safe deposit box, or hidden around the house.	Zero—and your cash becomes less valuable due to inflation.
Money in financial institutions. This includes checking accounts, savings accounts, money market accounts, and certificates of deposit.	For current rates on these types of accounts, talk to your financial institution or go to www.bankrate.com.
U.S. Treasury bills, notes, and bonds. When you buy these securities, you are lending money to the federal government. Depending on the type of security, your investment matures in one to ten years or more. The income from these investments may be free from state income taxes.	The rates change with the economy, but sometimes do not keep up with inflation. For current rates, go to www.finance.yahoo.com/bonds. For the results of recent auctions visit www.treasurydirect.gov.
I and EE/E savings bonds. EE/E savings bonds pay a fixed interest rate while I savings bonds are indexed to inflation.	For current rates go to www.treasurydirect.gov.
Individual stocks. These include any publicly traded stock.	The average return for "blue chip" (large cap) stock investments has been between 10% and 11% since the mid 1970s, typically 6–7% more than inflation. For historical information on an individual stock, go to www.morningstar.com.

Rates of Return, continued	
Type of Asset or Investment Product	**Rate of Return**
Corporate bonds. These are loans to corporations. High quality (highly rated corporate bonds) are considered low risk, while junk bonds (lower rated) are a moderate to high risk. Their ratings are usually tied to the solvency of the company.	Returns depend on bond rating and term but, in general, corporate bonds have average yields lower than stocks and less volatility. For current rates go to www.finance.yahoo.com/bonds.
Municipal bonds. When you buy a municipal bond, you are loaning money to a government entity. Municipal bonds have yields below corporate bonds but have the added advantage of being free from federal (and sometimes state) income taxes. This is attractive for people in higher federal tax brackets, especially those who live in states with relatively high income taxes.	Returns depend on the bond rating and term. For current rates go to www.finance.yahoo.com/bonds.
Mutual funds. Mutual funds invest in stocks, bonds, and other securities. You can buy a mutual fund that focuses on an index, industry, sector, or region of the world or country. Mutual funds have varying risks. Large company stock funds and high quality stocks are a lower risk than small- and mid-size company stock and international stock funds.	The average mutual fund yield is less than the average stock because of management and other fees. Studies show that only the top 10–20% of mutual funds beat the stock market. You can review historical returns for a particular mutual fund in its prospectus or annual report. Or, visit www.morningstar.com for useful information about all mutual funds.
Real estate. This includes your primary residence, vacation homes, and investment properties. As realtors like to say, it is all about "location, location, location" when making these investments. Appreciation varies widely by region of the country and the type of property.	Home price increases were strong in 2002–06 but have since leveled off or decreased. Talk to a realtor for information about the local market.
Collectibles. This category includes investment alternatives not covered above, such as coin and stamp collections, antique furniture, classic cars, jewelry, and art.	Returns vary widely but can be high for a knowledgeable investor.

How Will Inflation Affect Your Retirement Plans?

Prices will continue to rise while you are retired. Inflation rates are the third great unknown.

Because of inflation, you can expect that your monthly expenses will increase each year during retirement. Your monthly income probably won't increase at the same rate. From 1913–2006, the rate of inflation averaged 3.43% per year. The average annual rates of inflation in recent decades were:

- 2.36% in the 60s
- 7.09% in the 70s
- 5.55% in the 80s
- 3.00% in the 90s, and
- 2.85% from 2000 through 2006.

If inflation continues to average around 3%, your living expenses will double every 24 years.

Planning for Inflation

Here are a few ways that some people deal with inflation when planning for retirement:

- Make major purchases, such as new furniture and a new car, before you retire.
- Spend less money than you have available during your early retirement years. This can be accomplished by being frugal or by making conservative guesses about your life expectancy and rates of return on your investments—in other words, by anticipating a longer life and less income.
- Plan to spend less money as you age. The living expenses of the average 75-year-old are about one-third of a person between the ages of 45 and 54.

Making Your Financial Projections: Three Steps

The rest of this chapter will help you complete some simple, yet useful, financial projections. As mentioned, you will use these projections to determine how much you can afford to invest in your retirement business and how much you will need to earn. Following this three-step process will lead you to the numbers you need to make your decisions:

Step 1: Get Organized

- Gather financial documents regarding all of your assets, debts, and living expenses.
- Make a decision about your life expectancy as well as that of your spouse or partner.
- Determine the estimated rates of return on your various investments, consulting your financial adviser or tax professional if necessary.

Step 2: Complete the Tools

- Work through the Tools in the rest of this chapter. You should complete each that applies to you, but you don't have to do them in order. You may find it easier to complete some of them than others, depending on the thoroughness and accuracy of your financial records. (This is a good time to fill in gaps in your record keeping, if there are any.)
- Some of the Tools ask you to project account balances or market values for your assets and liabilities on the date you retire. Make your best guess for these, taking into account the amount you have now, how long it will be before you retire, changes you anticipate making, and the rate of return you expect on your investments.

- Keep in mind that your monthly income and expenses may change during retirement. For example, you may have payments on a home mortgage when you first retire, but plan to pay it off after two or three years. For simplicity, the Tools allow for only one monthly amount per item, so use an average, or enter the full amount of the payment to get the most conservative result in the final Tool.
- You will find the Tools for this chapter on the CD-ROM in two formats; we recommend that you use the *Excel* worksheets if possible. The total for every column in the *Excel* worksheets is calculated for you. This eliminates math errors and makes it easy for you to make revisions. In addition, the worksheets for your retirement plans and liquid assets help you evaluate various options for generating monthly income. (See Appendix A, "How to Use the CD-ROM," for detailed instructions on using the *Excel* worksheets.) If you don't want to use the *Excel* worksheets, you can complete the Tools by performing the math calculations manually or by entering projections you may have from a previously prepared financial plan.

Step 3: Review and Revise

- The last Tool in the chapter provides a financial summary of all your information. (If you use the *Excel* worksheets, you will find the summary Tool there as well.) Review your work with a critical eye. It is very easy to make errors, so be sure to double check your figures.
- Revise your financial projections as necessary, but be realistic. Do not make changes just to get the figures you desire.

Forecasting Investment Income: Be Conservative

Forecasting the income you will receive from any investment means you have to deal with the uncertainties of life expectancy and rate of return. Let's take a look at how Joe and Ellen dealt with this issue:

Joe is 60 and his wife, Ellen, is 55. They both recently retired. Joe is an optimist who is in good health and believes he will live at least another 25 years. Ellen is more of a pessimist and feels she will be lucky if she lives 25 more years—none of her relatives have ever lived to be 80. They decide to be conservative and make financial decisions based on at least one of them living for 30 years.

Joe and Ellen have invested $80,000 in three value oriented mutual funds and believe these investments will earn an average of 7%, but for planning purposes they decide to be conservative and use an estimate of 6%. Using an *Excel* Tool on the CD-ROM, they determine that they can expect to receive a monthly payment of $480 for 30 years. At the end of 30 years, the balance of their account will be zero.

Notice that Ellen and Joe built two cushions into their estimates. They used life expectancies that are longer than the government figures and they used a rate of return that is less than the rate they actually expect. They want any financial surprises during their retirement years to be pleasant ones.

We suggest that, like Joe and Ellen, you take a conservative approach to your projections. If you want to minimize the chance of running out of money, add a few years to your life expectancy and lower your expected investment return by a percentage point or two. This will give you the cushion that you may need.

Retirement Plans: IRAs, 401(k)s, Social Security, and More

There are many types of retirement plans—and you might have more than one. In this section, we want you to examine every account designed to provide income to you during retirement. These can be placed into one of three categories:

- employer-sponsored plans, such as defined benefit plans, profit-sharing plans, 401(k) plans, and 403(b) plans
- individual retirement savings plans outside of your employment, including traditional and Roth IRAs, and
- Social Security.

RESOURCE

More information about types of retirement plans. If you need to learn more about retirement plan basics, the IRS website offers an article that explains the plans mentioned above and many more. Visit www.irs.gov and search for "types of retirement plans." You can also turn to the following resources from Nolo:

- *IRAs, 401(k)s & Other Retirement Plans*, by Twila Slesnick and John C. Suttle
- *Social Security, Medicare & Government Pensions*, by Joseph L. Matthews and Dorothy Matthews Berman.

Perhaps you diligently read your retirement plan statements and know exactly how they work and what your payouts will be—but for many of us, that's not the case. Plans can be confusing and you might be uncertain about what to expect in the future. If so, you will have some research to do before you complete the Tool in this section.

Gather your most recent statements and explore the following questions, consulting a trusted financial adviser if necessary:

- At what age are you eligible to receive benefits?
- At what age must you begin to receive benefits?
- How does your retirement age affect your monthly benefits?
- How are your monthly benefits calculated?
- Will your monthly benefits change after you start receiving benefits?
- What benefits will your spouse or partner receive if you die first?
- Will your benefits change if you go back to work?
- Are your benefits taxable on your federal and state income tax returns?
- Do you have the option to roll your account balance into a different type of retirement plan?

Social Security

If you have worked as an employee or have been self-employed for at least ten years, then you are most likely eligible for Social Security benefits. Each year, you should receive a statement from the Social Security Administration (SSA) with details of your account, including:

- whether you are eligible for benefits
- Social Security earnings for each year you worked
- the monthly benefit you will receive at a variety of ages, and
- how to apply for retirement benefits.

Your annual statement will probably answer any questions you have, but if you need more information about Social Security, visit the SSA website at www.socialsecurity.gov.

In the following Tool, you'll list the account balance you expect for each retirement plan on the date you retire. This amount will depend on how much you have in the account now, how long it will be until you retire, your salary, and how much you expect the retirement plan to earn. You might want to consult your plan administrator or a financial expert to make your best guess for each plan.

Be careful when dealing with lump sum distributions and rollovers into other accounts—for example, rolling over the balance of a defined benefit plan into an IRA. Be sure to list each balance just once. Also, note that your information from the Social Security Administration won't include a projected account balance, so that cell is marked as "N/A" on the worksheet.

The *Excel* worksheet on the CD-ROM can help you evaluate various options for taking monthly income from your accounts. You can type in factors such as your earnings rate, the number of years over which you will withdraw funds, and your cushion amount to see how your expected monthly income changes. (See Appendix A for more information about using the CD-ROM.)

YOUR RETIREMENT PLANS

	Projected Account Balance at Retirement	Projected Monthly Income in Retirement
Defined Benefit Plan		
Profit-Sharing Plan		
401(k)		
403(b)		
IRA		
Roth IRA		
Other		
Social Security	N/A	
Total		

Liquid Assets: Cash, Stocks, and Bonds

Don't try to buy at the bottom and sell at the top. It can't be done except by liars.
—BERNARD BARUCH

You need to have some liquid assets—cash, stocks, and bonds—in the mix of your retirement finances. Why?

Unplanned fluctuations in your income and expenses are a fact of life. Your income may be lower than planned because of a vacancy in your rental property, slow sales in your retirement business, or a low rate of return on your IRA account. Your expenses increase when the transmission goes out, the hot water heater starts leaking, or an errant softball breaks your window. When you need cash in a hurry, you will rely on your liquid assets—cash and investments that can quickly be turned into cash.

Using the following Tool, you will organize information about your liquid assets—including account balances at retirement and expected monthly income. As with all the Tools in this chapter, be as thorough as possible when providing figures, but do remember that these are only projections. Don't get bogged down trying to figure out whether an account balance will be $10,500 or $10,600. Make an educated guess.

If you don't have an estimate of monthly income from your financial adviser, or if you want to test various scenarios, use the *Excel* Tool on the CD-ROM. As with your retirement accounts, it will help you evaluate various options for taking monthly income.

YOUR LIQUID ASSETS	Projected Account Balance at Retirement	Projected Monthly Income in Retirement
Cash		
Checking Accounts		
Savings Accounts		
Certificates of Deposit		
Shares of Stock		
Bonds		
Mutual Funds		
Other		
Total		

Spend a few minutes reviewing your results. If you aren't happy with your answers, think about making some changes in your savings and investment plans. You may want to increase the amount of money in your liquid investments or change the types of investments you own. And the sooner the better. If there's still time before you retire, increasing the rate of return on your liquid investments by a percent or two can make a significant difference when you start drawing down the funds.

Real Estate: Your Home and Investment Properties

In this section, you will look at your real estate assets. In case you're not sure what to include here, keep in mind that real estate (sometimes called "real property") is generally defined as land and any property that is built on the land. So a barn, house, shed, or even a fence would be considered real estate.

Equipment and vehicles parked on the land or in a building are not real property; they are classified as personal property, which you'll consider in coming sections. Also, note that in this section you are accounting for real estate you own. The costs associated with any real estate for which you pay rent are considered housing expenses and are covered later in this chapter.

Due to uncertainties in the real estate market, making projections of your real estate investments is more complicated than for most other assets. You need to estimate the future value of your real estate, any associated loan when you retire, and additional monthly expenses. Projected monthly expenses include loan payments, property taxes, insurance, utilities, maintenance, and homeowners' association dues.

For income property, you also must estimate monthly income during retirement. The goal is to help you focus on monthly cash flow from your real estate investments that you can use during retirement.

Real Estate Strategies

When projecting your real estate investments upon retirement, you might wish to consider a variety of strategies. For example, depending on your particular needs, you could:

- Refinance your primary residence to lower your monthly payments; it is easier to qualify for a mortgage while you are still working.
- Sell your present home and purchase a less expensive one to lower monthly property taxes, utilities, and maintenance.
- Pay off some real estate loans early to lower your monthly payments in retirement.
- Sell some real estate to help pay for retirement.
- Purchase additional rental properties.

If you have a financial adviser, you'll want to discuss your options in detail. Be sure you carefully evaluate the tax implications of any changes you are considering.

To complete the following Tool, you'll need to be familiar with two terms:

- **Equity.** Your equity in real estate is simply the difference between its market value and the balance of any loan on the property. Hopefully, this is a positive number. If you buy real estate with a very small down payment and market values fall, you may have negative equity.
- **Net cash flow.** Your net cash flow is what you get when you subtract your monthly expenses from your monthly income. The number will be negative for your primary residence and may be positive or negative for investment properties. Investors often hope that the increase in their equity in the property will more than offset their negative cash flow.

YOUR REAL ESTATE

Step 1: Complete all four columns and calculate the totals.

	Projected Market Value at Retirement	Projected Loan Balance at Retirement	Projected Monthly Income in Retirement	Projected Monthly Expenses in Retirement
Primary Home			N/A	
Vacation Home				
Timeshares				
Investment 1:				
Investment 2:				
Investment 3:				
Investment 4:				
Total				

Step 2: Calculate projected equity.

(Equity = Total Market Values – Total Loan Balances)

Your Projected Equity = $________________

Step 3: Calculate projected net cash flow.

(Net cash flow = Total Monthly Income – Total Monthly Expenses)

Your Projected Net Cash Flow = $________________

Now that you have a sense of the projected cash flow from your real estate investments, here's something to think about: Many people, while employed, aren't concerned if they have very little, or even negative, cash flow from their real estate investments. They aren't relying on their real estate investments to generate money to pay living expenses. The logic is that the appreciation of the properties more than makes up for the negative cash flow. But this scenario may not be acceptable when you retire; you may need cash from your real estate at that point.

Gary and Sharyn have concentrated their investments in rental properties because they feel that real estate is safer than the stock market and that the returns on bonds are too low. In addition to the home where they live, they now own four single-family houses and a duplex. Gary enjoys the maintenance work and Sharyn is very good at keeping the financial records and interviewing prospective tenants.

The rental income more than covers their expenses, but they take out very little cash for themselves each month. Instead, almost all their monthly profit goes into improving the properties. However, their five investment properties have been appreciating in value. Gary and Sharyn would like to purchase more properties after retiring from their jobs but are concerned that, even though their investments appreciate in value, the cash flow is minimal. They, like many real estate investors, are "land rich and cash poor" and worry about needing more cash flow during retirement. Their accountant puts together a plan to sell one of their properties and use the proceeds to pay down the debt on the remaining properties. This will allow them to increase their cash flow during retirement.

Collectibles and Other Income-Producing Assets

You have already looked at what are likely to be your major assets: retirement plans, liquid assets, and real estate. This section covers a variety of other assets that can provide you with income. The following checklist is to jog your thinking and help you identify any of these assets you may own.

Collectibles and Other Assets

Some common items which may figure into your retirement plans include:

- coin collections
- stamp collections
- firearms collections
- contract payments from a sale of real estate
- cash value of a life insurance policy
- ownership interest in a family business
- royalties from a book or song you wrote, or from other intellectual property.

Here are some common ways collectibles and other assets can help fund your retirement:

- Life insurance can be borrowed against or surrendered to obtain cash.
- Assets such as contracts or royalties can be renegotiated or sold.
- Stamp and coin collections can be liquidated for cash.
- An ownership interest in a family business can be sold.

Alice is a freelance writer for several industry magazines and a couple of business clients. She has always worked for herself. This independence has allowed her to choose the jobs she wants, but the financial rewards haven't been great. She has a small amount of liquid assets and an IRA but no other retirement plans.

Alice's situation doesn't sound too good—so far. However, she published a book ten years ago and receives royalty payments every six months. Alice also has a collection of gold coins that she inherited from her grandfather.

Her retirement goal is to continuing writing, on a part-time basis, for the rest of her life. She would like to devote her time to writing another book rather than on projects for trade publications and business clients. She hopes the royalties will enable her to achieve her dream. If Alice is still short of funds, she plans to sell some of her gold coins for additional cash.

You might not be planning to use your collectibles as a steady source of monthly income. More likely, your thought is to sell stamps or coins when prices are good or you need a little extra money. However, the upcoming Tool is designed to take into account monthly income, not intermittent income, so you'll have to make your best guesses. If you don't plan to sell your collectibles, enter zero in the monthly income column.

YOUR COLLECTIBLES AND OTHER ASSETS

	Projected Market Value at Retirement	Projected Monthly Income in Retirement
Notes and Contracts		
Royalties		
Life Insurance (Cash Value)		
Interest in Family Business		
Coin Collection		
Stamp Collection		
Other Assets		
Total		

Toys and Necessities: Boats, RVs, and Other Vehicles

This section covers assets that are purchased for pleasure (boats and RVs) or as a requirement of daily living (vehicles and furniture). These items are the necessities and toys of your life. They play a role in your retirement plans in three important ways:

- They are often purchased with a loan that requires a monthly payment.
- Their value usually decreases over time.
- You must usually pay to maintain and operate them. (These expenses will be accounted for in a later section.)

These items rarely have a positive impact on your retirement financial situation: The money goes out but it doesn't come back. Classic cars and antique furniture may be some exceptions to this rule. If you own a 1957 Mustang or an antique roll-top desk, surely these items are increasing in value. You should include any personal asset that you consider an investment in the "Collectibles and Other Assets" Tool, above.

The items you own now may be different than what you'll own when you retire. And these items will not remain constant during retirement. Your cars, RVs, and other items will wear out or your needs will change as your retirement lifestyle develops. And your monthly payments will not necessarily remain the same in retirement, but your current payments are a good starting point for looking at the future.

We suggest you use this Tool to account for all assets with a value of at least $2,500.

YOUR TOYS AND NECESSITIES

	Projected Market Value at Retirement	Projected Loan Balance at Retirement	Projected Monthly Payment in Retirement
Vehicle 1			
Vehicle 2			
Vehicle 3			
RV			
Boat			
Household Items			
Other			
Total			

Take a few minutes to review the Tool you just completed. If you feel uncomfortable with the figures you see then consider making some changes. You may not be sure if you can afford the monthly payments during retirement. You will have a better feel once you have completed the remaining Tools in this chapter.

Other Liabilities: Credit Cards and Other Debt

Annual income twenty pounds, annual expenditure nineteen nineteen and six, result happiness. Annual income twenty pounds, annual expenditure twenty pounds ought and six, result misery.

—CHARLES DICKENS, *DAVID COPPERFIELD*

Many Americans spend in excess of their income. How? Plastic! Americans love to pay with plastic. This is nothing new. As the quote above shows, people have been living beyond their means for many years. Currently, it is estimated that the average American has $8,562 in credit card debt and pays $1,000 per year in finance charges. Only 40% of folks pay their balances in full each month, and 20% of all credit cards are maxed out.

In this section, we'd like you to list any liabilities that are not secured by assets, such as real estate and vehicles. These are known as "unsecured" debts. In addition to credit cards, examples are a signature loan from your credit union or loans from family members. When you retire you may still be paying off your existing unsecured debts as well as incurring new ones.

Managing Unsecured Debt

If you have more unsecured debt than is comfortable, it's time to take action. If you don't, your level of debt is likely to remain unchanged—or worsen—during retirement. Here are a few tips:

- Adjust your spending. Putting even a little more money toward paying down your debts can make a surprisingly big difference over time.
- Pay off some of your unsecured debt before you retire by refinancing your house or obtaining a home equity loan—loans secured by real estate are less costly than unsecured loans.
- Refinance some unsecured debt with a debt consolidation loan. But use caution—make sure the debt consolidation loan will actually be less costly.

Nolo offers two books to help you take control of your debt: *Solve Your Money Troubles* and *Credit Repair*, both by Robin Leonard.

Estimating your postretirement debts can be challenging. Here are a few hints to help you through the process: If you have definite plans to change the amount of these unsecured debts then make your estimates according to those revised figures. If your payments have been fairly steady in recent years, you might want to assume that you will maintain that level during retirement. If your liabilities have varied considerably, you should give some serious thought to what they will be after you retire.

YOUR OTHER LIABILITIES

	Projected Amount Owed at Retirement	Projected Monthly Payment in Retirement
Notes and Contracts		
Unsecured Loans		
Credit Card 1:		
Credit Card 2:		
Credit Card 3:		
Other		
Total		

Spending Money in Retirement

In previous sections you listed your monthly payments for real estate and personal property assets. You have also calculated your monthly payments for debts and other liabilities. In this section, you will complete the picture of where your money goes by taking a look at other monthly living expenses. This is an important step to help you determine how much money you will need from your retirement business. (You will identify the expenses associated with your retirement business in a later chapter, after you've chosen your best business idea.)

Here are brief explanations of the categories of retirement expenses covered by the following Tool:

- **Housing.** You have already accounted for monthly expenses for real estate you own. Here, you should include expenses for property you rent, including your monthly rent payments and items such as utilities, maintenance, and insurance.

- **Vehicles.** You have already accounted for monthly loan payments on your vehicles. In this Tool, you should include insurance, gas, oil, tires, and repairs and maintenance.
- **Travel.** This category includes a wide variety of expenses, such as airfare, rental cars, cruises, tours, lodging, and campground fees.
- **Recreation.** This is also a rather broad category that includes music, movies, education, club memberships, reading materials, ski lift passes, rounds of golf, concerts, and other types of recreation or entertainment.
- **Food and drink.** Include the cost of groceries as well as items purchased in restaurants and bars.
- **Health care.** This category includes office visits to doctors, dentists, and other health care providers, as well as medical insurance, eyeglasses, prescription medication, vitamins, and supplements.
- **Income taxes.** This category includes federal income taxes, state and local income taxes and self-employment tax. Property taxes have been included under real estate.
- **Other.** Include expenses not already covered; such as clothing, toiletries, gifts, sports equipment, hobby equipment, charitable contributions, care for your pets, and your computer and related items.

Many people assume their expenses will be less when they retire. That sounds good, but don't assume you can easily cut your expenses. Remember that while you're losing some work-related expenses, you may be gaining lots of time in which to spend money. Fundamentally, your spending habits have evolved over many years—and change doesn't often come easy. If you want to save money, you'll need to a real plan to make it happen.

The goal of this Tool is to list monthly expenses that you think you will incur in the future, not monthly payments for past expenses. So look ahead, and remember to account for the effects of inflation. (See "Planning for Inflation," above, for more information.)

YOUR RETIREMENT LIVING EXPENSES		
	Estimated Present Monthly Expenses	**Projected Monthly Expenses in Retirement**
Housing		
Vehicles		
Travel		
Recreation		
Food and Drink		
Health Care		
Income Taxes		
Other		
Total		

Financial Summary

The financial summary is a review of the previous Tools in this chapter. You may have filled out something similar when applying for a loan from a financial institution. By completing it, you will learn two important pieces of financial information:

- **Your net worth.** Your net worth is the difference between your assets and your liabilities. For most people, their net worth is reduced during retirement as they take monthly income from their assets. Your net worth is the source of money from which you will fund your retirement business; more about this after you complete the Tool.
- **Your net cash flow.** The difference between your income and expenses will indicate whether you can expect a positive or negative monthly cash flow during retirement. After you finish the Tool, you will discover how this figure will help you select your retirement business.

YOUR FINANCIAL SUMMARY

Step 1: Complete all four columns and calculate the totals. You don't need figures for any field marked "N/A" (not applicable).

	Projected Values of Assets at Retirement	Projected Balances of Liabilities at Retirement	Projected Monthly Income in Retirement	Projected Monthly Expenses in Retirement
Retirement Plans		N/A		N/A
Liquid Assets		N/A		N/A
Real Estate				
Collectibles		N/A		N/A
Toys and Necessities			N/A	
Other Liabilities	N/A		N/A	
Retirement Living Expenses	N/A	N/A	N/A	
Total				

Step 2: Calculate projected net worth.

(Net Worth = Total Values of Assets – Total Balances of Liabilities)

Your Projected Net Worth = $________________

Step 3: Calculate projected net cash flow.

(Net cash flow = Total Monthly Income – Total Monthly Expenses)

Your Projected Net Cash Flow = $________________

Review and Revise

Take a few moments to review all of your Tools using the following guidelines:

Check the details. Check your work for errors. If you're making these projections with a spouse or partner, leave the checking to whoever is most likely to see the Tools through fresh eyes.

CD-EXTRA!

Help on the CD-ROM. If you've been using the *Excel* worksheets to track your financial data, you'll want to look at the "Financial Details" worksheet in the Money Tools file on the CD-ROM. It automatically lists every line item from all the Tools in this chapter and will help you quickly identify errors.

Think about your net worth. This information will tell you how much you have available to invest in your business. Remember that if you sell some of your assets as a means of financing your retirement business then you have reduced your net worth. The assets you sell are no longer available to provide your estimated monthly income, so you'll need to revise your figures accordingly.

Evaluate your net cash flow. Understanding your projected monthly cash flow is critical to selecting the business opportunity that will meet your financial needs. If you have enough cash flow, then you have no pressure to earn money from your retirement business. You may want to earn money, but profit may not be the most important consideration when choosing a business. If your cash flow is negative, however, you'll need to earn some money. Earning power will be an important factor in choosing your retirement business.

Make revisions. If you have discovered some errors or want to change some of your retirement assumptions, revise the appropriate Tools. Don't make any changes with the sole purpose of increasing your net worth and net cash flow. It is important to use figures based on reality, not wishful thinking.

MY PROFILE

Completing Your Profile. Good job! You have taken a thorough look at your present financial situation and what you expect when you retire. And you're almost done with your Profile. Turn to it and complete the final section. It summarizes:

- how much you will invest in your new business, and
- how much income you want to earn from your business.

Your responses should be based on the math work you did in this chapter and your attitudes about money. Choose dollar amounts that reflect your financial reality and your approach to risk.

As soon as you finish, you're ready to take the next step—brainstorming great business ideas.

Generate Great Business Ideas

Maybe you're a born entrepreneur. If so, generating business ideas is second nature to you. It's exciting and maybe even addicting. Everywhere you look you see great business opportunities just waiting for someone to jump in and make a bundle.

Most of us aren't like that. We wonder how in the world entrepreneurs come up with their ideas. If that sounds familiar, Step 3 of this book is for you.

The key to developing business ideas is twofold: Look often and look everywhere. One reason your cousin Fred comes up with great business ideas is because he's always looking for them. He probably rejects 49 out of every 50 ideas he gets. Those are the ones he never tells you about. Finding business ideas requires exercising your "entrepreneurial muscles." The more you look, the more ideas you'll find and the easier it will become.

But just looking often isn't enough. You also need to search widely, considering all types of businesses. For example, suppose you'd like to build your retirement business around your interest in books. Your first business idea might be to own a bookstore. But you already know that, these days, independent bookstores are struggling and it might not be your best option. Fortunately, there are many other possibilities. You could be a consultant on rare editions, or restore bindings and covers for worn and torn classics. You could sell books by local authors at the state fair, offer an online editing service, or start a mobile bookstore, selling across the country as you travel in your RV.

Chapter 7 gives you a framework for thinking about possible businesses you could start. We talk about retailers, wholesalers, manufacturers, and service providers, and we introduce some established business arrangements, such as franchising, that often suit retirees. Thinking about general types of business will broaden your perspective and help you generate more and better ideas.

Then, because it's easiest to look for business ideas in the context of what's familiar to you, **Chapter 8** helps you examine your work experience, interests, skills, and experiences as a consumer. You might discover that you want to open a yoga studio or a bed and breakfast, or use your artistic skills painting murals on buildings. You'll also look at trends and think about whether you'd like to copy what other, successful businesses are doing.

So you don't lose any important insights, we'll show you how to keep track of all your business ideas on index cards using our recommended grid.

If you already have more business ideas than you know what to do with, or if you only have one idea but are pretty sure that's what you want to do, you could skip this step. But, who knows? Using the Tools in these chapters just might lead to an even better business idea—the one that's just right for you in retirement.

CHAPTER

7

Types of Businesses You Can Start

In the beginner's mind there are many possibilities.
In the expert's mind there are few.
—SHUNRYU SUZUKI

Looking everywhere means examining possible business ideas from many different angles. It means thinking beyond traditional retail storefronts. It means considering more than consumer products. What about offering a service to businesses instead of individuals? What about manufacturing products rather than buying them?

This chapter helps you search for business ideas by exploring two questions:

- Will you provide products or services?
- Will your customers be individuals or organizations?

You'll see that, by mixing and matching the answers to these questions, you can generate a wide range of ideas.

Bill owned a small business selling flares and other road safety supplies at venues like road races and county fairs. One day, he learned that power companies and all governmental agencies, including police and fire departments, were required to have safety supplies in every vehicle. Bill put the required supplies into a compact, user-friendly kit and started selling to organizations as well as individuals—a very profitable move.

Every business sells products or services and many offer a combination of the two. For instance, building a backyard deck uses carpentry services but also leaves the customer with a new product. Selling and installing garage door openers provides a product with a service attached.

Don't worry about fine-tuning distinctions between services and products as you search for business ideas. The important thing is to explore all types of businesses so you can find the one that's right for you.

What's in It for Me?

As you search for business ideas, think about your potential customers. They'll always be asking, "What's in it for me?"

That means you must consider the problems they may have and how you can solve them. What do they need and how can you get it for them? Perhaps local businesses need to modernize their storefronts. You could sell and install colorful awnings. If they already have awnings, maybe they need them cleaned.

Walk in the customers' shoes and see things from their perspective. This can greatly expand your list of business ideas.

Recording Your Ideas

As novelist John Steinbeck said, "Ideas are like rabbits." Start developing business ideas and you'll find they multiply. But if you don't write them down and keep them handy, your great ideas might scatter into the thickets of your daily worries and be lost forever.

As you work through this chapter and the next, use some 3" x 5" index cards for recording business ideas. Keep them in your car, purse, or briefcase—or even in your pockets—where you can grab a new card when the next brainstorm hits. You can jot down your business ideas any way you like, but you may find it helpful to think in terms of what you would provide and to whom. You can use a grid like the one below. Write your business idea in the appropriate quadrant. For example, if your idea is to provide document storage for small medical facilities, you would record this in the quadrant of providing a service to organizations.

BUSINESS IDEA CARD

Your Customers		
What you provide:	**Individuals**	**Organizations**
Product		
Service		

Expect to have plenty of ideas that you won't want to pursue—and a few that just seem nuts. For example, you might think of being a caricature sketch artist at parties but immediately worry that there's no market for a business like that. Don't let such concerns stop the flow of ideas. For now, suspend judgment. Even if an idea seems way out of line, write it down. You never know where it might lead.

Selling Products to Individuals

Sell to their needs, not yours.

—EARL G. GRAVES

We've noticed that many people searching for business ideas look first at consumer products. After all, you buy food, clothing, toys, and toiletries all the time, so that seems like a logical place to start. However, selling products to people can be a hard road. The competition is fierce and has intensified with the explosion of Big Box retailers—large, stand-alone stores such as Wal-Mart, Target, and Staples—and the advent of online sellers like Amazon. These large retailers compete on price and that's not a game most small businesses can win.

Does this mean it's impossible to make a profit selling products to individuals? Of course not. But you have to strategize carefully. Here are some things that small businesses do to succeed:

- **Specialize.** Perhaps your best customer is not the average consumer. Some people are attracted to better quality, uniqueness, or specialized applications. The sales volume for specialized products often is too low to interest larger businesses, so that leaves a great opening for small business owners. For example, you can buy outdoor grills at Home Depot and Lowe's, made by well-known companies such as Char-Broil and Jenn-Air. How could a small business compete? The Traeger Company does it with unique technology. Their grills burn wood pellets and attract customers seeking an alternative to charcoal or gas.

- **Add value.** Small businesses can sell the same products as bigger competitors by adding something of value to what the customer buys. For example, you might provide a more personalized shopping experience, better technical support, or free installation.
- **Sell locally made products.** There are some products which, by their nature, are easier to produce and sell locally. Examples include fruits and vegetables sold at farmers' markets, nursery stock, custom drapes, and flower arrangements. Also, there is a small but loyal market segment that prefers to buy from local producers as a way to help the local economy or the environment. Serving your local market with local products can be a great strategy.

Chris owns a store selling television and stereo equipment. He lives in a small town with no large retailers, but it's only 30 miles to the nearest Sears, Best Buy, Costco, and Wal-Mart. Chris can't carry as many brands as his larger competitors and he can't match their prices, yet his business does well. He competes by adding value to the products he sells. Chris delivers a new television or home theater, sets it up to suit his customers' preferences and needs, and is right there to answer questions, not only when he installs the equipment but for years to come.

- **Sell follow-on products.** These are the things people need in addition to a primary product. For example, it's unlikely that your business will be manufacturing cameras. However, camera owners require many other products and services: photo developing; specialty print products, such as family calendars and greeting cards; accessories, such as straps, bags, and cleaning cloths; photo archiving software; picture frames; photo storage boxes; restoring and digitizing old pictures. As you generate business ideas, keep follow-on products in mind. They can greatly widen your search.

- **Buy wisely.** Some small business owners build their successful retail business around great buying strategies. They know exactly what and how much to buy. They know where to get the right products and how much to spend. Businesses that require buying expertise can be great for collectors—selling gems, baseball cards, or stamps. If you love checking out what's new on the market, comparing prices, monitoring quality, and looking for bargains, look for business ideas where smart buying is a big part of the process.
- **Be a small-scale manufacturer.** Your business could buy raw materials and components and manufacture final products rather than buy them. This is the way many retirees turn their hobby into a business. Mark buys shafts and club heads and builds golf clubs in his garage. Claire buys reeds and grasses for the baskets she weaves. It's usually difficult for small businesses to manufacture large volumes, so look for specialized products that work well with smaller volumes.

John and Ellen import decorative items and clay pots from Mexico and sell them at their Arizona store. Similar items are available from other retailers, but John and Ellen offer better quality and a slightly lower price. They can do this because they know their merchandise well and have great skills as buyers.

- **Operate a job shop.** For most small manufacturers, it is much easier to work as a job shop than in continuous production. Continuous production means cranking out lots of look-alike products. In a job shop, you work on specific customer orders and the products are typically customized. For instance, most printers work as job shops, printing only what the customer orders, when they order it. And working as a job shop can ease one problem many people have when turning their hobby into a business: If you don't have to make too many identical products, you won't lose the sense of pride and satisfaction in craftsmanship you've always enjoyed.

RESOURCE

Go to *Entrepreneur* for business ideas. *Entrepreneur* magazine has a website entirely devoted to exploring new business ideas. You can search for ideas by industry and scan lists of business ideas to see if any pique your interest. Check out www.entrepreneur.com/businessideas.

Selling Products to Organizations

Your retirement business could sell products to organizations rather than to individual consumers. These types of businesses are usually called wholesalers or distributors and their customers are other businesses, government agencies, or nonprofit organizations.

Selling products to organizations can make for a great retirement business, but keep in mind that it can be difficult if you target large companies. Retirees usually find that their contacts from working in a large corporation dry up quickly. And the practical concerns can be overwhelming: Big companies often need such large quantities, quick turnarounds, or specialized treatments that it can be impossible for small business owners to meet their demands. Selling products to government agencies and larger nonprofits can also challenge small business owners with mountains of red tape and detailed, time consuming procedural requirements.

Larry will soon retire from his career as a postal carrier and build custom furniture and cabinets. For years, he's done this as a side business after work and on weekends. He already knows the kind of order he doesn't want to take. A few years back, he received an order for 46 interior doors. It was a profitable deal, but producing the doors was a chore: He had to speed things up by sawing until all 46 doors were sawed, sanding until all 46 doors were sanded, staining until he could barely stand the sight of another door. Continuous production mode didn't work well for Larry. He missed the joy he usually felt when turning raw materials into finely crafted furniture.

For these reasons, you might prefer to focus on products you could sell to small- and medium-sized businesses. They are sometimes overlooked by major suppliers.

If you're interested in selling products to organizations, think about the following strategies:

- **Sell products the customer will use internally.** These can range from office supplies to promotional items to hand tools to a catered dinner for the company Christmas party. You can sell to the organization as a whole or to smaller groups within it. For example, you might sell customized screen-printed T-shirts for softball teams at the manufacturing companies in your city.
- **Make components.** Your product might be just one part of the final product your customer is making. For example, you might make fused glass buttons to be added by designers to custom-made suits and gowns. Great business opportunities have come from major manufacturers who need components that are too few or too specialized for the company to do in-house.
- **Build prototypes.** Companies developing new products often need a prototype or model. For example, an organization may need an example of new packaging materials or ergonomic tools. It may not know how to build what it wants or it might not have the equipment to do it. Also, a company will most likely need only one or two of each prototype and that is an inefficient use of their time and facilities. If you are skilled with milling equipment, building prototypes can be a challenging and rewarding business.
- **Sell products the customer will resell.** You could sell products to wholesalers and distributors, letting them sell to the ultimate consumer. This is particularly effective for unique or high-priced products—for instance, custom-made leather purses or hand-painted ceramic bowls—or if the market is widespread. A distributor often has marketing and distribution connections that would take you many years to develop. Be careful, however, not to promise more product volume than you can deliver.

Selling Products Online

As you're searching for business ideas, consider selling products online. The Internet has changed the face of business dramatically in a relatively short period of time. E-commerce (buying and selling products and services online) has exploded. The Census Bureau of the Department of Commerce estimated that U.S. retail e-commerce sales for 2006 were more than $108 billion. The Forrester Research Company predicts that total internet sales (to people and to businesses) will reach $329 billion by 2010.

Starting an online business can be particularly advantageous for retirees who don't want to be tied to the structured time schedule of a bricks-and-mortar store. And you can work at home, saving money because you won't pay rent.

Of course, the downside is that the business could take over your home, especially if your products are large in size or many in number.

A successful online product business starts from the same guiding principle as any other business: You must answer the customer question, "What's in it for me?" Too many aspiring online business owners skip this step, thinking that if they just put products on eBay or build their own Web storefront, people all over the world will click right onto the site and the money will roll in. If it were that easy, we'd all be millionaires!

RESOURCE

Ideas for online businesses. To peruse a list of possible online businesses, try *101 Internet Businesses You Can Start from Home: How to Choose and Build Your Own Successful e-Business,* by Susan Sweeney (Maximum Press).

CD-EXTRA!

More information about selling online. Once you've chosen a business idea, you can learn more about whether or not selling online will benefit you. Look for the bonus article "Is Selling Online Right for Your Business?" on the CD-ROM.

Providing Services to Individuals

Providing a service can be a particularly good niche for small businesses. As we mentioned above, competition from big retail stores sometimes makes it difficult to sell products to individuals. With services, the competition tends to be from smaller, local companies, so it's much easier to enter the market and compete on even ground.

Service businesses generally provide either technical or professional expertise. Technical service providers work with tangible items—think plumbers, auto mechanics, gardeners, welders, tailors, window cleaners, delivery services, dog groomers, interior decorators, computer technicians, and closet organizers. Professional expertise providers work primarily with knowledge, not things. Consulting and training are the two most common professional service businesses started by retirees, but the category also includes professions such as insurance brokers, income tax preparers, wedding planners, attorneys, personal trainers, and credit counselors.

As with product businesses, there are strategies you can consider when searching for service businesses to start:

- **Bundle.** Your business could offer a single service to customers—for example, swimming pool maintenance—and that might be good enough to make it work. But what if you offer more than one service? Along with pool maintenance, you might provide yard care and patio power washing. Your business could be a one-stop shop for everything customers need for their outdoor living area. Bundled services are convenient for customers and a great way to distinguish your business from your competitors.

- **Partner with a product seller.** You could team up with a product seller and offer a related service. For example, retailers of custom windows and doors often do not install them. Instead, they keep a list of contractors and direct the installation work to them. Look for products a bit too complicated for most people to install or service themselves. Sometimes, there's more money to be made from servicing products than from selling them.
- **Get licensed or certified.** Hundreds, if not thousands, of occupations require state or local licenses. For example, in many states, anyone can operate a lawn-mowing business, but only those with a special license can install sprinkler systems. Check out the websites for your state and local governments. Perusing their lists of occupations requiring licenses or certifications is a great way to expand your search for service business ideas. In addition, educational institutions offer certifications for many skills. These can range from phlebotomy (how to draw blood) to welding. Some of these programs are a requirement for getting a license, but others are strictly voluntary. Completing one of these programs can give you a competitive advantage in your business. Being a certified Web designer, financial planner, or golf instructor could establish your credentials and make it easier to start your service business. To find certification programs in your area, check the websites and course catalogues for local colleges and universities.

Curt used to run a machine shop for an auto parts store. He could build new parts, grind rough edges, or fix broken welds. However, with the growth of nationwide franchised auto parts stores, this combination of a retail store with a machine shop has mostly gone by the wayside. Nevertheless, Curt saw a need for this service and successfully teamed up with several local auto parts stores, which now come to him for machining work.

How Will You Deliver Your Products or Services?

One way to distinguish your business and build a competitive advantage is to think about how you deliver your products or services to customers. You have two basic options: customers either come to you or you go to them.

Customers may come to a retail store but those who shop from a mail order catalogue or online get to stay home while the product comes to them.

The same can be true for service businesses. For example, golf carts serve as a second car in some Arizona retirement communities. Some businesses will repair your cart if you bring it to their shop, but a few savvy business owners have differentiated their businesses by making house calls; they will come to you to make the necessary repairs. As you search for ideas, keep delivery options in mind.

RESOURCE

If you have a type of business in mind. Many publishers offer books for starting up specific businesses. One of these books might be right on topic for you—or you might find a business idea just by reviewing the titles. Here are a couple of places to start:

Entrepreneur publishes a "Startup" Series. Each book covers a particular business—from event planning to automobile detailing, from import/export businesses to travel services. You can find a complete list at www.smallbizbooks.com.

Globe Pequot Press publishes a "Home-Based Business" Series, with books on catering, interior design, writing, owning an antiques business, and many more. Find their booklist at www.globepequot.com. Click on the "Special Interest" tab and then choose "Business, Technical & Professional" category from the list on the left.

Providing Services to Organizations

Your retirement business could offer services to organizations. For example, if your technical skill is heating and air-conditioning repair, you may wish to focus on complex industrial sites rather than home repairs. If you have worked 25 years as a legal secretary, you may want to organize court documents for small legal firms on a contract basis.

Consider the following strategies as you search for business ideas:

- **Serve outsource needs.** Outsourcing refers to one organization hiring another to do what might otherwise be done internally. It's a huge part of our economy, creating many opportunities for new businesses. Organizations outsource everything from hiring employees to shipping the final product. That said, just as it can be difficult to sell products to big businesses, it also can be difficult to be an outsource service provider if an organization's demands exceed the service you can provide. Look for outsourcing opportunities with small- and medium-sized businesses.
- **Remanufacture.** Remanufacturing involves repairing or remaking worn-out or defective products or components. Although this involves working on products, it is actually a service since you are only working on your customer's products, not selling them yourself. Manufacturers don't like to deal with remanufacturing internally because they are set up to make new products. These types of opportunities are usually very specialized, so to make it work you will probably need significant industry experience and strong ties to potential customers.

RESOURCE

More books for business ideas. There are a number of books that offer loads of business ideas. Some offer more help than others when it comes to starting a business, but it can be enlightening just to peruse the possibilities. Here are two that focus on home businesses:

The 200 Best Home Businesses: Easy to Start, Fun to Run, Highly Profitable, by Katina Jones (Adams Media Corporation), includes the pros and cons of starting different businesses and helps you estimate start-up costs.

Best Home Businesses for People 50+, by Sarah and Paul Edwards (Tarcher), features 70 comprehensive profiles of businesses particularly well-suited for Boomers.

Providing Services Online

If you're interested in starting an online business, take a look at services you might offer. Of course, many services don't lend themselves well to e-commerce. It's hard to replace a car windshield without actually touching the car! But there are some services that do not require your physical presence with the customer. Online education reaches millions of students. Computer programmers don't ever have to meet their customers face to face. Even some astrologers offer their services only online. Think about your service business ideas and whether they'd work online.

Franchises and Other Business Arrangements

You can expand your search for business ideas by considering some specific ways of doing business that often work well for retirees. These include franchises, authorized dealerships, selling on commission, and multilevel or network marketing.

Franchises

Franchises are undoubtedly popular—there are more than 600,000 franchise outlets in America. Almost every fast-food restaurant you can think of is operated as a franchise, but there are hundreds of other types of businesses that use this system, such as Jackson Hewitt Tax Service,

Jiffy Lube, and UPS Stores. Some franchises are particularly suited for home-based businesses, such as Budget Blinds, ServiceMaster Clean, and Candy Bouquet.

Generally, franchises are businesses that allow the franchisee (that would be you) to use something from the franchisor: a trade-name, a system of operating, access to a distribution network, advertising. In return, the franchisee pays fees to start up and continue the business. There are plenty of pluses but also some downsides to opening a franchise; we list the most common just below.

Franchises: Pros and Cons

Here are some advantages and disadvantages to consider if you're thinking of buying a franchise.

Advantages

- You can use the franchisor's established management and operational procedures rather than having to devise your own.
- You can get instant product or service recognition rather than spending the time and money to build it yourself.
- You might receive professional help selecting a location.
- You can benefit from nationwide advertising programs.
- You might have access to financing programs offered by the franchisor.

Disadvantages

- You will pay upfront and continuing fees to the franchisor.
- You may be required to purchase materials from specified suppliers and have little control over what you buy and how much you pay.
- You may feel like you're not really in charge of your own business because of tight operating standards imposed by the franchisor.
- You may have conditions to meet, like standards for cleanliness, timeliness, or profitability. Failure to do so could risk termination of your franchise.

RESOURCE

More information about franchises. Even if you have no interest in buying a franchise, they are a great source of business ideas. There are many websites about franchises. Surf these sites and you may find the right business idea for you.

- www.betheboss.com
- www.franchiseopportunities.com
- www.franchisesolutions.com.

Authorized Dealerships

An authorized dealer (also known as a distributor) sells another company's products. Sometimes the dealer is restricted to selling only products from that manufacturer. Dealers usually sell to retailers or directly to the public. Dealerships often include geographic territory restrictions. An authorized dealership differs from a franchise in a couple of important ways: A franchisee generally gets more operational support and training, and the franchisee can use the franchisor's trade name—like Subway or Budget Blinds—as their own.

Although many manufacturers work only with bigger companies as their authorized dealers—think of new car dealerships and appliances—there are dealership opportunities for small business owners. For instance, Nancy is an authorized dealer of a popular brand of surgical gloves. She supplies medical offices within a 50-mile radius of her home.

SEE AN EXPERT

Talk to a lawyer before you sign on the dotted line. There are many laws governing the sale and operation of franchises, dealerships, licenses, and other established business arrangements. (These arrangements are often grouped under the heading "Business Opportunities.") The laws are designed to protect you from fraud and deception by unscrupulous sellers. Unfortunately, the myriad of rules can also lead to information overload and make it difficult to evaluate these organizations as potential business ideas. Seek the advice of a knowledgeable attorney if you are interested in a franchise, dealership, or similar arrangement.

Commission Sales

A commissioned salesperson works as an independent contractor rather than as an employee. Under this type of arrangement, your earnings would be a percentage of sales dollars, rather than an hourly wage or monthly salary. Some common industries for this option are insurance, real estate, financial services, automobiles, RVs, boats, furniture, appliances, and electronics. Commissioned sales arrangements usually require little, if any, upfront costs. If you're a skilled salesperson, commissioned sales can give you great flexibility and big profits.

Multilevel or Network Marketing

To be sure, people have had many bad experiences with multilevel or network marketing organizations, especially those devised as pyramid schemes (also known as Ponzi schemes) in which the only goal is to sign up new members. But other network marketers are legitimate businesses utilizing a sound structure for commissioned sales. These can be a good source of business ideas.

Reputable network marketing organizations, such as Amway, Mary Kay Cosmetics, and Tupperware sell quality products and services to their customers at competitive prices. Associates earn money from selling products or services themselves and from the sales made by associates they recruit into the business, but not from the act of recruitment alone.

It is important to evaluate the requirements to join a multilevel marketing organization. Be on the lookout for exorbitant joining fees or requirements to make a significant investment in inventory.

RESOURCE

How to check out business opportunities. *Entrepreneur* provides lists of top franchises, business opportunities, and multilevel marketing organizations on their website: www.entrepreneur.com.

CHAPTER

Six Sources of Business Ideas

The average person has four ideas a year which, if any one is acted on, would make them a millionaire.

—BRIAN TRACY

The last chapter guided you through the types of businesses to consider as you look for retirement business ideas. That framework will help you start your search. But it's a big world out there and just thinking in general about products or services may not get you to your final idea. How can you sift through the millions of possibilities? You need to focus your search. That's what the Tools in this chapter will help you do.

There are six common ways to find business ideas. They may come from:

- your employment
- your interests and hobbies
- your skills
- your consumer experiences
- copycatting, and
- trends.

Your business idea could spring from any one of these sources, so it's a good strategy to explore all of them and generate as many ideas as possible. As you work through the Tools, keep in mind that your business might be selling a product or providing a service to individuals or organizations; that you could buy or manufacture products; that you could bring the customer to you or go to the customer. And

Judy found her business idea when her husband received a gift basket for his birthday. What a disappointment! The basket was sloppily prepared, had nothing of real interest included, and Judy learned later that it had cost a small fortune. Judy was very skilled at flower arranging and enjoyed shopping for gourmet food items. "I can do better," she thought. And she did.

Sandy discovered her best idea while visiting a friend who snowbirds to an Arizona retirement community. "Leaving this home in the hot summer could be a problem," her friend said. "Thank goodness there's a business here that takes care of my home while I'm gone." Sandy lived in an Oregon resort community with many summer residences. Did those folks need assistance during the winter? Yes, they did. Sandy copied the housesitting idea for her own community.

don't forget online businesses, franchises, and commission work. The more you practice generating business ideas, the easier it will get.

As you work through the Tools in this chapter, keep your 3" x 5" index cards handy. Write down every business idea that comes to you. Don't worry if the idea sounds far-fetched. You'll have a chance to refine your ideas a little later.

Source #1: Your Employment

The best way to get a good idea is to get a lot of ideas.

—LINUS PAULING

The majority of business owners got their idea from their past work experience. This is particularly true for the many retirees who have become consultants. After all, contacts, credentials, and insider knowledge can make it easier to find work and get it done.

Identifying business ideas from your current or past employment is a matter of looking for weak links: gaps in the processes, seasonal tasks that do not justify a full-time employee, products in quantities too small for a large company to focus on. What is inefficient? What would make the customer's experience easier? Faster? Cheaper? What do customers want that they can't get? You can use this Tool for your current employment and as many of your past jobs as you wish.

Joe and Shirley spent their careers in education, with Joe working at the local community college. Upon retirement, they moved to a fast-growing part of their state and Joe noticed that a successful training program he'd organized in their old city was missing in their new locale. Joe and Shirley combined their teaching and administrative experiences to start a training business, tapping Joe's community college contacts for promotion and access to facilities.

IDEAS FROM YOUR EMPLOYMENT

My employment as: ____________________

1. What everyone always said made their jobs more difficult:

   ____

2. The company could save a lot of money if only:

   ____

3. Something the company doesn't do because it says the profit margin is too small:

   ____

4. What the company should do, but can't because everyone is too busy:

   ____

5. What the customers always asked for:

   ____

6. What the customers always complained about:

   ____

7. The company needs this task done, but it doesn't justify a full-time employee:

   ____

8. The company needs this product only occasionally, or in such small quantities that it's inefficient to make it in-house:

   ____

Source #2: Your Interests and Hobbies

Not enthused about building a business based on your work experience? Well, perhaps you can develop business ideas using the interests you identified in Chapter 1. Many businesses sprang from a love for arranging flowers, collecting rocks, playing golf, or dancing.

Think about the times when you've been immersed in a favorite activity. Have you ever thought to yourself, "You know, this process would be so much easier if there were a better …"? Or, "Gee, if I could just take one of these and merge it with one of those, it would be so much faster or cleaner or cheaper?" Chances are that if you're frustrated, others feel the same way. Find a solution to the problem and you've got a business idea.

This next Tool helps you use your interests to find business ideas. You can repeat this Tool for as many interest areas as you wish.

Dan knew he wanted to keep working after retiring, and his love for sailing drew him far from his previous career as an accountant. For a year after retiring, Dan learned all he could about the sailing industry. He worked as a laborer building boats, attended trade shows, interviewed sailing enthusiasts, and scoured catalogues, always searching for the right business opportunity. He found it as a freelancer writing articles about sailing for trade publications.

IDEAS FROM YOUR INTERESTS

Interest area: ______________________________

Whenever I am involved in this interest area, I wish:

1. I had this product or raw material:

   ____

2. I had this tool:

   ____

3. I had this knowledge:

   ____

4. I had this service:

   ____

Whenever I am involved in this interest area, it is difficult to:

5. Do this:

   ____

6. Find or buy this:

   ____

7. Learn about this:

   ____

Source #3: Your Skills

In Chapter 4, you listed your worker and owner skills. You could build your business around any one of them. It's generally easier to come up with business ideas based on your worker skills: an auto mechanic opens his own repair shop, a bookkeeper starts a payroll service, a French teacher becomes a tutor, a police officer becomes a security consultant.

But don't ignore your owner skills. Recall the discussion in the previous chapter about outsourcing. Businesses outsource all manner of activities, and your organizational skills could fit perfectly with their needs. For example, if you've been a human resources manager, your business could help organizations recruit executives. Or, if you're a retired administrative assistant, you could help companies organize their filing systems and paperwork. Don't restrict your search for business ideas to the industry in which you've worked. Organizational skills are needed for every type of business, nonprofit group, and governmental agency.

And don't shy away from business ideas just because you don't have all of the necessary skills right now. You can learn new skills!

Use the next Tool to consider the types of businesses you could start with your worker and owner skills. Feel free to list skills you plan to acquire as well as those you already have. Remember to think about all types of businesses: selling products or providing services to individuals or organizations.

Corporate downsizing forced **Denise** to retire early from her bank job, but she still needed to earn some money and wasn't ready for a full-time rocking chair. "But what kind of business could I start?" she asked, "The only two things I know how to do really well are cook and sew." Six months later, Chef Denise served her first catered luncheon.

Denise already had all the cooking skills she needed to start her business, but she had no experience with the owner skills: how to price a catered luncheon of baked salmon for 75 people, how to shop for 140 pounds of meat for beef stew, how to market a catering and personal chef business. She found an education program about the business side of catering and gained the owner skills she needed to open her business. "I absolutely love everything about this business: shopping, developing recipes, cooking. I even love cleaning up. This is the most fun I've ever had working and I still can't believe that I can actually make money just doing something I love."

IDEAS FROM YOUR SKILLS

My skill: ____________________

This skill could be used for selling these types of products to individuals:

____

____

____

This skill could be used for selling these types of products to organizations:

____

____

____

This skill could be used to provide these types of services to individuals:

____

____

____

This skill could be used to provide these types of services to organizations:

____

____

____

Karen's experience was similar to Denise's, except she already had the organizational skills she needed but lacked the technical skills. Karen owned an antique store in the small town where she had lived for years, but she dreamed of opening a bakery. Friends and family scoffed at her dream. What did she know about baking? Karen agreed. She needed to learn. At the young age of 70, she enrolled in a culinary institute and enjoyed every minute of her training.

TIP

Let Your Fingers Do the Walking. Don't ignore a readily available source of business ideas. Pick up the yellow pages and turn to various sections related to your employment, interests, or skills. Art is your passion? What categories are included in your phone book? You might find art galleries, art instruction, art restoration and conservation, art supplies, artists, and arts organizations—any one of which might lead you to a business idea. Do this for as many of your interests, jobs, and skills as you wish.

You can also search by surfing the Internet, although you might want to refine your search criteria carefully or you could end up wasting time digging through irrelevant and unwanted Web pages. For example, we searched for "art supplies" and got 32,700,000 pages, but "antique brass art easels" whittled it down to 85,800 pages—still too many, but those listed first were directly on point.

The yellow pages and Internet are also handy for identifying your competitors and learning which businesses may be missing from your community.

Remember to record any business ideas on your index cards.

Source #4: Your Consumer Experiences

Surely you've had consumer experiences where you've shaken your head in disbelief. Perhaps you've even walked out of a store or written a letter of complaint. The good news about these encounters is that your negative consumer experiences could give you a business idea.

On the other hand, what about those wonderful moments when everything works perfectly, and you feel like hugging your salesperson, bragging to everyone you know about this fantastic product you bought, or writing a thank you note to the business owner? Perhaps you can take what was so good about your experience and duplicate it in your business, even if you don't offer the same product or service.

Think about some of your positive and negative consumer experiences and complete the following Tool.

IDEAS FROM YOUR CONSUMER EXPERIENCES

My positive consumer experience:

____

The reason it was such a great experience:

____

What made the experience so great could also be helpful when people buy these products or services:

____

My negative consumer experience:

____

The reason it was such a bad experience:

____

People may have bad experiences like mine when they buy these other products or services:

____

I could do the following to change an experience like mine from bad to good:

____

Susan had 45 minutes for her lunch break. She usually brought lunch from home, preferring her own cooking to fast-food restaurants or cafeterias, but one morning she was running late and dashed out of the house without her lunch. At noon, she went out to buy a meal. It took ten minutes to drive, another five to find a place to park, another ten to stand in line and order. By the time she got her food, there was little time to eat. What a hassle! This negative consumer experience was the seed for Susan's business idea—a mobile soup deli in a van parked conveniently near one of the biggest and busiest companies around.

Source #5: Copycatting

Many ideas grow better when transplanted into another mind than in the one where they sprang up.
—OLIVER WENDELL HOLMES

More than 25,000 new products are brought to market each year. That's 486 per week, 69 per day. If you think that's impressive, consider that a new business is born in the United States every 11 seconds. That's 86,400 per day. Obviously, most new businesses aren't selling a new product. Nor are they inventing a new type of service. Instead, they're copycatting.

Most of us aren't inclined to invent new products or services, and even if we were, the odds of making money from an invention are extremely poor. So, small businesses usually sell products or services that already exist somewhere in the marketplace. Copycat business opportunities come from bringing an idea from another geographic region to your home town, taking a local idea elsewhere, or copycatting locally.

Peggy had a very demanding job and led a busy life. Even though she wrote appointments on her calendar, it was still hard to juggle her commitments, so she greatly appreciated the reminder post cards and phone calls from her dentist's office. And that became the basis of her business idea: She contracts out as a personal secretary for several clients, keeping their calendars and reminding them not just of upcoming business meetings, but also birthdays, anniversaries, and their next dental appointment.

A few years ago, **Laurie** was jazzed about her business idea. "I just got back from Seattle," she said. "There are drive-thru espresso stands popping up everywhere. We don't have anything like that here in Oregon. I'm going to open one." Laurie imported her copycat business idea and it was great timing—espresso now runs like rivers through almost every Oregon town.

Bringing a Copycat Idea Home

Great business ideas may come to light when you travel. What's popular in another city that's not available in yours? If you find an intriguing idea, you might be able to copy it at home.

Taking a Copycat Idea Elsewhere

What's available in your city that's not available in another? Of course, taking your copycat idea to another city can be problematic if you have no intention of moving. It's pretty hard to open a dance studio in Nevada if you live in New York! But location is not a big issue for some products and services. Perhaps it's an online business you can conduct anywhere. Or, maybe the business is seasonal. If you plan to sell Hawaiian shaved ice at summer fairs in Idaho, you don't need to live there the rest of the year. You also can start a business that requires occasional business trips.

Going someplace soon? Take the time to check out possible businesses. Peruse the local newspaper. Listen to the local residents. Visit the Chamber of Commerce and ask what's new and what's hot.

And if you plan to move, you'll want to think about businesses where you live now that do not exist where you are going.

Use the next Tool to help you think about copycat business ideas.

Terry was skilled at cleaning optical equipment. Most optometrists needed his services only once or twice per year. He didn't need to live in California to serve that market; he just lined up clients and hit the road for a few weeks at a time.

There already were several drive-thru espresso stands where **Kelly** lived, but she successfully copycatted that business idea by being the first to add a particular convenience for the customers: service windows and drive-up lanes on both sides of the stand. Service was faster and lines shorter and it was an easy approach for both eastbound and westbound drivers.

IDEAS FROM COPYCATTING

When I visited ______________________________

1. It seemed like this business was on every street corner:

   ____

2. There was this great store/product/service that I don't think we have at home: ______________________________

   What was so great about it was: ______________________________

3. The newspapers were full of stories and advertisements about:

   ____

4. It seemed like everyone was talking about:

   ____

5. It was so strange. I noticed that they don't have:

   ____

6. I heard people complain that they don't have:

   ____

7. We have much better ______________________________ at home.

8. This seemed to be new and exciting there: ______________________________ . Back home, we've already gone through that, and these products and services became really popular because of it: ______________________________

Copycatting Locally

Copycatting locally works just like bringing copycat ideas home from your travels, but you don't need to leave town. It's a matter of offering the same or similar products or services as other local businesses, but doing it better. You'll be going head-to-head with these competitors, so you'll need an advantage—something that makes customers want to come to you. For example, think about better customer service, faster delivery, lower prices, or higher quality. Copying a local business is a bit more difficult than offering a completely unique product or service, but it can be done.

Look and Listen

Good business ideas are often discovered by observing and listening. Mark is a great example. He was at a Super Bowl party. Bored with the lopsided game, Mark noticed the women at the party admire a woven handbag his date had bought in Indonesia. He asked the women why they liked the bag so much. Not long after, he flew to Bali to purchase handbags, and his business has been thriving ever since.

Go to an event, gathering, or store related to one of your interests. Watch the other people there carefully. Do patterns emerge? Anomalies? For example, if community theater is your passion, observe the audience coming into and leaving the theater. If drag races are your thing, go to a race and watch the people. Is someone wearing or carrying something everyone else covets? Is everyone complaining about an inconvenience? Extolling the virtues of some new gizmo? If they aren't saying much to help you—ask. What bugs them? What do they like? What do they need or desire? Use your index cards to write down any ideas.

Source #6: Trends

I believe we are on an irreversible trend toward more freedom and democracy—but that could change.

—DAN QUAYLE

You probably know someone who is financially independent because they were the first in your area to open a type of business that really took off. Maybe they were selling computers before the big box stores got into the act and then moved on to video rentals before Blockbuster came to town. Then they found the next big thing, always with a knack for knowing what's next.

Evaluating trends and focusing on what's coming next is a great way to find business ideas. Of course, just identifying a trend doesn't make it profitable or lasting. When looking at trends, you're predicting the future and that is surely fraught with danger. Your predictions may be wrong. Or, your evaluation of a trend might be absolutely spot on at the moment, only to have something happen that changes its direction in a flash. Still, considering trends may help you decide what to do—or not to do—so you don't want to ignore them completely.

You can find business ideas by looking at trends in the general population or marketplace. For example, suppose you recognize that more and more grandparents are raising their grandchildren.

Janice got the idea for a home health care business when she noticed two related trends. First, she became aware of the increasing number of older people living at home. Second, Janice knew that many nurses were aging and getting ready to retire. She learned that many of these nurses would like to work part-time, but that they wanted out of the administrative and bureaucratic atmosphere found in most hospitals and doctors' offices. They wanted to devote their hours to patient care. That was the clincher. Janice established procedures that met the nurses' needs and together they now successfully serve the home health care needs of hundreds in their city.

What opportunities does this trend create? Perhaps you can create a magazine for these grandparents, day care with hours to match their needs, look-alike sweatshirts with funny sayings, or counseling services.

You also can develop business ideas by focusing on trends specifically related to your interests, skills, and work experience. That's what the upcoming Tool will help you do. This can be easier than working with population or marketplace trends in general. You are probably very knowledgeable about coming changes in those arenas where you spend your time and money.

As a schoolteacher, **Doug** noticed significant growth in the number of parents home-schooling their children. He investigated the learning materials available to these parents and found that reading and math were pretty competitive areas, but that there was a lack of materials in science. Doug and his wife, Ann, developed computer learning resources for science, adding a special touch that tapped one of their interests: They composed and performed songs to accompany the learning modules.

Countertrends

Often a trend leaves behind countertrends—and excellent business opportunities. Consider, for example, recent changes in the music industry. Downloadable music and iPods have rocked the music industry but left behind a nostalgia market for record players and records. Suddenly, that old Iron Butterfly album gathering dust in a closet is a treasure again. Countertrend products and services often serve small markets, so they fit a small business very well.

Trends Versus Fads

There is no reason for any individual to have a computer in his home.

—KEN OLSEN, PRESIDENT, DIGITAL EQUIPMENT, 1977

What products and services will be popular next year? How about five years from now? We live in a world in which a movie star, fashion item, or restaurant that was popular only a short time ago is rarely mentioned today. How do you account for these rapid shifts when looking for business ideas?

Consider whether a change is truly a trend or just a fad. A fad is here today and gone tomorrow. Customers are very passionate about faddish products for a relatively short period of time. Pet Rocks, lime green clothing, and Beanie Babies were all very popular once. Although establishing a business around a fad can be profitable in the short run, staying in business requires coming up with the next fad and the next. Timing is everything. You can capitalize on a fad only if you catch it in the beginning. And, some fads never reach many parts of the country.

Trends have staying power. Clothing moved away from fabrics requiring special laundering and ironing to wrinkle-free materials. Digital photography has substantially displaced film. Cell phones are now used worldwide and pay phones are harder to find. Some products, like personal computers, were initially called a fad but proved to be the wave of the future. Timing is always important in business, but less so with a trend than with a fad. You don't have to be first out of the blocks with a product or service that has staying power.

Use the following Tool to summarize trends you see in relation to your interests, skills, and work experience. (Repeat it as many times as you wish.) Let's say you'd be overjoyed to build your retirement business around your love for gardening. What gardening trends do you see? An increase in hybridization allowing greater plant diversity in extreme climates? A return to cultivation of nonhybridized heirloom plants and vegetables? The aging of the vast majority of avid gardeners? Smaller yards needing more efficient use of garden space? Any one of these trends could lead to a business idea, so keep your index cards at hand.

IDEAS FROM EVALUATING TRENDS

My interest area, skill, or work experience:

____

I am aware of these trends:

1. ____
2. ____
3. ____

The trends I've identified may create a need for these products or services:

1. ____
2. ____
3. ____

Choose Your Best Business Idea

You've got business ideas. You've completed your Retirement Business Profile. Now it's time to bring it all together. In this step, you will set yourself up for success by purposefully choosing the retirement business that's right for you.

Chapter 9 helps you whittle your business ideas down to a reasonable number. Then, you'll use an easy rating system to identify your top five ideas. The idea that best matches your Profile is your number one business idea.

But you're not done yet: You need to look a little closer to be sure your favorite idea will work. It may sound great, but you won't want to launch the business unless the numbers make sense. Can you produce enough chocolate-covered popcorn balls or prepare enough tax returns to make a profit? Will enough customers want to buy your product or service?

Chapter 10 walks you through four reality checks to help you determine whether your business idea is feasible. You'll complete simple calculations to estimate how much money you'll need to start the business and how much money you can expect to make. If your calculations show that your idea is a winner, you'll know you've picked the best retirement business for you.

CHAPTER

Select Your Number One Idea

If you can control the process of choosing, you can take control of all aspects of your life.
—ROBERT F. BENNETT

This chapter shows you how to evaluate your business ideas and choose the one that fits you best. If you've already got an idea that you love, this chapter still has something to offer: It will help you make sure your idea is in alignment with your Retirement Business Profile.

Here's how you'll zero in on your best idea:

- Get ready to choose by reviewing your Profile.
- Identify your top five business ideas.
- Choose your number one idea.

When considering business ideas, try not to be biased in your evaluations. It's very easy to fall in love with a business idea, even if strong evidence indicates that it's not right for you. And we all have selective hearing when the truth means letting go of something in which we've invested our time, energy, and enthusiasm. But it's better to come to terms with a mismatch before it's too late. If the Tools in this chapter indicate that you need to go back to the drawing board for your business idea, then back you should go. You may learn that your idea will work if you change it just a little. Or, you may need to channel your efforts in a totally new direction.

While you want your business to match your wants and needs, you should also be on the lookout for unreal expectations. Even your best business idea is unlikely to line up perfectly with your Profile. That just doesn't happen very often. If it does, pat yourself on the back and thank your lucky stars that you've found the perfect business opportunity. But don't worry if perfection doesn't happen. The goal is to do the best you can.

Maggie loves dogs. It was her dream to open a kennel, but the more she investigated and learned about the legal requirements, the more expensive and troubling the idea became. So she settled on a variation of her original idea. She now has a dogsitting business, taking her services to the dogs rather than bringing the dogs to her.

Get Ready

How long has it been since you completed your Profile? Perhaps you haven't looked at it since you started gathering business ideas. Take some time to review it, and revise it if you need to. You don't have to be overly precise or excruciatingly thorough. Just make sure that your Profile still reflects you and your desires.

Jan always thought she'd spend most of her retirement hours at her sewing machine, happily quilting. Still, she knew she would need some extra income so she was also thinking of starting a business. She originally wrote in her Profile that she wanted to spend only 20 hours per week on her business, and she listed money as her primary motivation. But a funny thing happened as Jan searched for business ideas—she got more and more excited about owning a business. The ideas just kept coming and her quilting projects sat untouched. She decided to really go after a retirement business and put her quilting on hold for a few years. She made significant changes to her Profile before moving on to choose her business.

Identify Your Top Five Business Ideas

Choosing between five alternatives is usually much easier than choosing between ten or 20. If you've got a whole stack of business idea index cards, it's time to make some cuts.

SKIP AHEAD

If you have five or fewer ideas. If you only have a few business ideas, you can skip this step and go right to the next section.

Go through your index cards and make two piles: ideas to consider and ideas to discard. When deciding what to toss, look first for those ideas that aren't likely to get off the ground. If you know it's not practical to buy a hot air balloon and offer rides at county fairs, that's an idea for the discard pile. But do note that this is a "gut check," focused on your feelings, not on accounting equations or an analysis of supply and demand. In the next chapter, you'll have an opportunity to get into the numbers for your chosen business idea.

The following questions may help you decide which ideas to keep and which to discard:

- Are you genuinely excited about the business idea?
- How confident are you that you can make it work?
- Would you be comfortable telling people about your business idea?
- Will your family and friends support the idea? If not, are you comfortable pursuing it anyway?

There is no magic number of "yes" answers needed to keep or discard an idea, but each "no" answer means you need to think carefully about whether to retain that idea or not.

Cut and cut again until you have reduced your number of business idea cards to five or fewer.

Target Your Number One Idea

When choosing between two evils, I always like to try the one I've never tried before.

—MAE WEST

Here's where all your hard work comes together. In one hand, you've got your top five business ideas. In the other, you have your updated Profile. The Tool below helps you use your Profile to evaluate your business ideas and choose the best one.

Your best business idea will be the one that aligns with your interests, goals, values, motivations—all the factors you spelled out in your Profile. You'll see that the Tool gives you five columns, one for each business idea you're considering. Use fewer columns if you have fewer than five ideas or if you're just checking out that one business you've already set your sights on. You may of course add columns to accommodate more business ideas, but remember that including too many could make choosing difficult.

The rows in this Tool correspond to each part of your Profile, except money and time. (You'll be looking at both of these in the next chapter.)

For each Profile factor, rate your business ideas using the following scale:

5 = Excellent alignment

4 = Very good alignment

3 = Aligned fairly well

2 = Somewhat aligned

1 = Not at all aligned

Be as honest as you can. And try not to jump to conclusions about which idea is best until you've considered all of the factors for each of your ideas.

Do note that this method assumes all factors are equally important to you. If one or more of the factors means more to you, consider increasing the weight you assign to those factors. For example, if alignment with your values is most important, you could multiply each of those ratings by two before adding up your totals.

When you are done, add up the score for each business idea and enter the amount in the Total row.

YOUR NUMBER ONE BUSINESS IDEA

How well does this business idea align with:	Business Idea:	Business Idea:	Business Idea:	Business Idea:	Business Idea:
My Interests					
My Goals					
My Motives					
My Values					
My Work Style					
Where I Want to Live					
My Skills					
Total					

Check out your results. The business idea with the highest score is best aligned with your Profile. That's your number one business idea.

But what if there isn't a clear winner?

If none of your business ideas scores a high rating, it could mean that you just haven't found the right idea yet and you should keep looking. Or, it could be that you're not really into this whole idea of starting a retirement business. That's okay—and it might even be a relief. But if money was your motive for starting a business, you'll need to consider how else to get the income you need. Maybe getting a part-time job is a better match for you. Or, maybe you need to stay in your current job a few more years and sock away extra cash.

If two or three ideas have similar totals, review your ratings and your "gut check." Is one of the ideas more exciting to you? You can also take more than one idea into the next chapter. That's when you'll look at the numbers to see whether the business makes sense financially. Differing answers to financial questions could very well help you choose between several ideas that seem appealing right now.

Perform Four Reality Checks

Reality is that which, when you stop believing in it, doesn't go away.
—PHILIP K. DICK

You've done it! You've found your business idea. What are you waiting for? Get out there and make it happen.

Not so fast. Not every business idea makes a good business opportunity. Before you invest your time and hard-earned savings into a new business, you should answer these four questions:

- How many customers do you need?
- How many customers can you serve?
- Can you compete?
- Can you finance your business idea?

These questions are your reality checks. Your business idea isn't likely to make good sense unless it passes each one, so be thoughtful about your answers. We suggest that you keep the following points in mind:

If you don't know, find out. Checking out your business idea requires some research. At this stage, you'll need answers that are reasonable, but not necessarily precise. Do enough investigation to make educated guesses.

Don't give up. If a reality check raises a red flag, it doesn't necessarily mean your business idea is doomed. You might have to tweak the idea: Find a new way to manufacture your goods, a new way to serve customers, a different way to finance your business. Look for ways around an obstacle before you throw out your idea, but heed the next point, too.

Be honest with yourself. Be open to hearing what you don't want to hear. If your reality checks raise serious doubts about your idea, don't ignore the results. You want to be successful—the one out of two new businesses that is still operating after 18 months.

Keeping Score

If winning isn't everything, why do they keep score?

—VINCENT LOMBARDI

Owning a small business is like playing a game: You need to keep score to know whether or not you are winning—in this case, meeting your goals.

How you keep score depends on the type of business you want to start. For many businesses, it makes sense to look at the number of customers served. Owners of businesses like convenience stores and restaurants often talk about the number of customers who made a purchase in a given time period.

But there are other options. Here are three common ones:

- **Billable hours.** This is the number of hours you can charge to your customers. Attorneys, CPAs, and other professionals sell their expertise by the hour and monitor their billable hours daily.
- **Projects.** Some business owners track the number of projects they can accept and complete. Consultants, building contractors, and writers often think of their work this way; they sell their expertise by the project.
- **Products.** Finally, you might choose to track the number of products your customers are likely to purchase. Retailers track products sold in order to know whether their items are selling and when it's time to reorder.

Because it's most common to keep score by number of customers, that's how we set up the Tools in this chapter. If a different way of scorekeeping works better for your business, by all means use it. Just substitute billable hours, or projects, or products whenever a Tool refers to customers.

Reality Check #1: How Many Customers Do You Need?

To be a successful business opportunity, your idea must profitably fill a market need. Even if making money isn't your primary motivation for starting a retirement business, it's doubtful you want to lose any. You've already stated in your Profile the amount of money you must earn and the amount you'd like to earn in your business. How many customers (or billable hours, projects, or products) do you need in order to reach your goal?

You can't know for sure whether your business will make the money you desire, but you can do some basic calculations to evaluate your chances for success. Here's what you'll do as you complete the Tools in this section (don't worry if you're not familiar with all of these terms; we'll define them—and explain why they're important—as we go):

- estimate your monthly fixed costs
- estimate your variable costs per customer
- estimate your average selling price per customer, and
- calculate your contribution margin per customer.

Using the figures from these four steps, you'll determine the volume required to meet your financial goals. This calculation will help you complete your first reality check: How many customers do you need?

Monthly Overhead: Your Fixed Costs

Fixed costs, often called overhead, stay the same each month no matter how many products you sell or how many customers you serve. Rent is a good example: If you pay $600 to rent an office, that monthly amount remains the same whether you have 20 sales or 200. For many small businesses, the majority of costs are fixed.

Even if a cost is "fixed," it's unlikely to stay the same forever. Your landlord may raise your rent to $650, or you may decide to move your business to your home. So "fixed" doesn't mean set in stone; it means that the cost won't fluctuate with changes in sales volume.

Here is your chance to estimate the fixed costs you will incur in a typical month. We've listed common costs, but feel free to add any others that relate to your business. If a cost will be paid only once or twice per year—for instance, insurance premiums—you can distribute the total cost equally to estimate a monthly amount. But don't include costs that will be one-time requirements of starting your business. You'll look at your start-up costs a little later.

YOUR MONTHLY FIXED COSTS

Fixed Costs	Monthly Amount
Advertising	
Office Supplies	
Rent	
Utilities	
Phone	
Internet	
Insurance	
Outside Accountant	
Legal Fees	
Subscriptions	
Dues	
Salaries and Wages	
Payroll Taxes	
Other	
Total Fixed Costs	

Variable Costs

Variable costs change with volume. Let's say you pay to ship your products to customers. The more products you ship, the more you'll pay. For example, if it costs $3 to ship to each customer, then 100 customers means you'll spend $300 and 200 customers means you'll spend $600. Or, perhaps you use subcontractors to help you with your consulting projects—so the more consulting projects you have, the more you pay for subcontractors.

Primary variable costs for most product-oriented small businesses are:

- costs of buying the products to be resold
- shipping costs, both inbound and outbound, and
- materials and supplies specific to a sale.

Common variable costs for service businesses are:

- materials and supplies specific to a sale
- sales commissions or subcontractors, and
- travel.

Deciding whether a cost is fixed or variable isn't always easy. Some costs may be mixed. For example, you may pay a flat fee per month for phone service (a fixed cost) and additional charges for long distance (a variable cost). You can try and split a mixed cost into its fixed and variable components, but make sure it's worth the trouble. If the total cost is insignificant, it's much easier to treat it as a fixed cost, using an average amount spent each month.

Use the Tool below to list your variable costs per customer.

YOUR VARIABLE COSTS

Variable Costs	Monthly Amount
Cost of Product	
Shipping Costs	
Materials and Supplies	
Travel	
Sales Commissions	
Subcontractors	
Other	
Total Variable Costs per Customer	

Pricing

The prices you charge will play a major role in determining how financially successful your retirement business will be. A word of caution: The majority of new business owners charge less than market rate for their products or services. They think that's the only way they will attract customers, but low prices don't guarantee customers and can make it very difficult to turn a profit. Choose a realistic price and don't sell yourself short.

To determine the financial feasibility of your business idea you need to choose an average price per customer (or billable hour, or project, or product). For example, you could estimate that each customer will spend an average of $85 per purchase. Of course, you may change your mind about pricing before actually starting your business, but make your best guess for the reality check.

Setting Prices

Before you set your prices, take a good look at the market for your product or service, paying particular attention to these four factors:

- **Costs.** You must set your prices to cover both fixed and variable costs and give you a profit.
- **Demand.** If you've got a hot-selling product or service, you'll be able to charge a bit more for it. Of course, the opposite is also true: If nobody wants what you're selling, you'll have to cut your prices.
- **Supply.** Products and services that are hard to come by fetch higher prices than those that are readily available.
- **Competition.** You don't have to beat your competitors' prices, but you don't want to charge a lot more, either. The amount of flexibility you have depends on how important price is to customers. It's bound to be more important for products and services that seem alike (undifferentiated), and less important if you're offering something unique.

Selling more than one product or service can complicate what may otherwise be an easy step. But remember that only estimates are required. If your business will offer many types of products or services, use a reasonable average price. For example, if you'll be offering five different products that normally sell between $20 and $30 each, you can use an average price of $25 when completing your reality checks.

You'll enter your average sales price in the Tool below when you estimate your contribution margin.

Terry planned to teach time management seminars. He noticed that his competitors charged between $130 and $180 for seminars similar in length to his. He could try to match the high price, but decided he didn't have the name recognition to make people want to come no matter what the price. However, he also believed he had some unique insights and techniques to offer, so he didn't want to be at the low end of pricing either. Terry decided to estimate a price of $150 per student.

Contribution Margin

This section helps you calculate your contribution margin from each customer. The contribution margin is your selling price minus your variable costs.

Why is it called the contribution margin? What does it contribute to? Three important things: The contribution margin pays your fixed costs, provides you with an income, and keeps your business growing through reinvestment.

Use the following Tool to calculate your contribution margin, then keep that number handy—you'll use it when you get to the final Tool in this section.

Let's continue the story of **Terry** and his time management seminars. He will charge each student $150. His major variable costs are a course manual for each student and the snacks and coffee he provides. He estimated these variable costs to be $45 per student. That means Terry's contribution margin is $105 per student. Terry will use the $105 per student to cover his fixed costs, pay himself, and invest in the growth of his business.

YOUR CONTRIBUTION MARGIN

Step 1: Enter your average sales price per customer: $__________ (A)

Step 2: Enter your variable cost per customer: $__________ (B)

Step 3: Calculate your contribution margin per customer: Sales price minus variable costs (A) – (B): $__________

The Number of Customers You Need

How many customers will you need in order to meet your financial goals? In this section, you'll find out by bringing together all the calculations you've just made.

Recall that your contribution margin (your average price minus variable costs) does three important things:

- It helps to pay your fixed costs.
- It provides you with money to take from your business.
- It leaves a profit to help your business grow.

And that's the order in which you must use the funds. It's critical that you cover your fixed costs before taking any money for yourself or attempting to grow your business. If nothing's left over after paying fixed costs, you'll get zero money out of your business.

Surely, that's not your goal. So this reality check helps you calculate how many customers you'll need to make the money you want from your business.

Mike is an auto broker. He visits local auctions, buys vehicles, fixes them up, and resells them. He estimates his contribution margin as $500 per car. His monthly fixed costs are $1,000 and he'd like to withdraw $2,000 from his business each month. Mike needs to sell six cars per month to cover his fixed costs and his withdrawals. If most people buy one car per year, then Mike must find 72 customers to meet his financial goals.

Refer to your Profile and the Tools above to complete your first reality check. Use the two amounts you indicated in your Profile after completing Chapter 6: the amount you must earn and the amount you'd like to earn.

CUSTOMERS NEEDED TO MEET YOUR FINANCIAL GOALS

Step 1: Enter your total monthly fixed costs in both columns.

Step 2: Consult your Profile and enter the monthly amount you must earn (first column) and the amount you'd like to earn (second column).

Step 3: Add (A) and (B) in each column to find the total of your fixed costs and desired income.

Step 4: In each column, enter your contribution margin per customer.

Step 5: Calculate the number of customers you must have each month to meet your financial goals.

	How Much I Must Earn	**How Much I'd Like to Earn**
(A) Monthly Fixed Costs		
(B) Desired Monthly Income		
(C) Total Fixed Costs and Desired Income = A + B		
(D) Contribution Margin per Customer		
(E) Number of Customers Needed Monthly = C ÷ D		

Sally is a graphic artist who designs logos for small business clients. She needs to earn at least $1,475 per month from her retirement business. Sally charges an average of $400 per client and her variable costs (materials and travel) average $20, so her contribution margin per project is $380. Her fixed costs are fairly minimal—$425 per month—because she works at home.

Sally's first reality check showed her how many logos she must design in a given month to meet her financial goals. Her fixed costs of $425 plus the income she needs of $1,475 means she must earn at least $1,900 per month. She divided $1,900 by her contribution margin of $380. The answer? She must design five logos each month to meet her financial needs.

If the number of customers you calculated strikes you as unrealistic or makes you uncomfortable, then review your estimates and see if you can justify changes to your prices or costs. But be realistic. Don't change the numbers for the sake of making your idea pass the reality check. If your original estimates still seem correct, you either need to tinker with your business idea or select a different one.

Reality Check #2: How Many Customers Can You Serve?

Even if you are on the right track, you'll get run over if you just sit there.
—WILL ROGERS

Your capacity to produce or sell your product, or to service your customers, is limited. Capacity challenges generally come in two flavors: time constraints and operational constraints. Your second reality check will consider both.

Time Constraints

Some new business owners are surprised to find that they don't have time to produce enough products or serve enough customers to make their endeavor profitable. This can happen to any business owner, but time challenges are especially common for service businesses, manufacturers, and building contractors.

When considering time constraints for your business, think about your skills inventory in Chapter 4. The more skilled you are at producing your product, providing your service, or managing

Howard used to work in construction, so self-employment as a home inspector made sense. He already had the licenses he needed, and he had connections in the community to send business his way. He examined his financial needs and set a goal for monthly earnings. But it didn't work. True, he got plenty of business referrals—the phone rang off the hook with new customers. But Howard learned that each home inspection absorbed so many hours that he could complete only a limited number of them, which meant his monthly revenue never met his goal.

your business, the less time it will take. Relating your skills to time constraints can point out areas in which you need to improve.

In addition, recall the discussion in Chapter 4 about the roles you'll play in your business: Unless you hire employees, you will be both the owner and the worker. As the worker, you must produce a product or perform a service for your clients. Many new business owners make the mistake of thinking only of their worker tasks when scheduling their time. But your owner tasks (such as marketing, administration, accounting, and planning) can chew up many hours. Be sure you take those hours into account when determining your capacity.

RESOURCE

Balancing your owner and worker roles. For more information and helpful advice about your owner and worker roles, read one of our favorite books: *The E-Myth Revisited*, by Michael E. Gerber (HarperBusiness). It walks you through the steps in the life of a business and gives great advice about working *on* your business, not just *in* your business.

TIP

Tackling Time Constraints. Small business owners often complain that there are never enough hours in the day. Here are some ways to relieve the pressure of time constraints:

- **Use technology.** Identify tasks that you could complete faster by using a better piece of equipment or new software.
- **Improve your skills.** Identify tasks where you could save time if you had more training.
- **Use other people.** Identify repetitive tasks that could be performed by an employee or by outsourcing.
- **Stay focused.** Take a hard look at everything you do; make sure your time is spent on essential tasks.
- **Raise your prices.** You will probably lose a few customers, but you may be able to make just as much money in less time.

Operational Constraints

We know of a successful bakery owner who has been approached by many would-be bakers about distributing their fantastic cookies. These are great, he'd say, but how many can you bake in your ovens each day? If they answered just a few dozen, he'd tell them they had a great cookie, but a lousy business.

Your ability to meet your financial goals might be constrained by operational problems, such as the size of your workshop, the maximum output of your machinery, or a limited supply of product or materials. Operational constraints are most important for retailers, restaurant owners, manufacturers, and building contractors.

What Are Your Capacity Constraints?

Think about your business idea. How many products will you be able to turn out? How many hours can you devote to clients? How many hours will each job require?

The following Tool helps you evaluate your capacity. If you don't know how long a job will take, seek the help of someone who provides a similar service. If you're not sure about the production capacity of the machinery you'll use, do enough research to learn the particulars. Of course, each job won't take an identical amount of time and effort. When making your calculations, rely on educated guesses and reasonable averages.

This Tool first focuses on your hours as a worker. Remember that you'll also spend time in your owner role. Go back to your Profile and, in the section

Trudy, a new restaurant owner, insisted on buying only the best when she located her new restaurant in a local strip mall. The result was a very attractive restaurant with high monthly fixed costs. She ran into trouble when she discovered that there wasn't enough space in the restaurant to seat the number of customers she needed to make her business work. She tried promoting take-out but there wasn't enough capacity in the kitchen to make meals for both dine-in and take-out customers. The physical capacity of her restaurant prevented her from achieving her financial goals.

from Chapter 5, find the number of hours per week you'd like to spend on your business. Multiply by four to convert that to hours per month. Then, look at the Profile section from Chapter 4 and find your estimate of the percentage of time you'll devote to your worker role. Multiply hours per month by your worker percentage and you'll have an estimate of your worker hours.

Now think about how much time you'll spend with each customer and you can determine how many customers you have the capacity to serve. If you have experience in your type of business, you probably can estimate time per customer fairly easily. Otherwise, consult with those who do have experience and get a reasonable estimate.

Cheryl wants to work no more than 40 hours per week in her housecleaning business. That's an average of 160 hours per month. Cheryl estimates that 25% of her time will be taken up with owner duties and 75% for worker tasks—so, she can spend 120 hours per month as a worker.

As mentioned earlier, your capacity might be constrained by something other than time. This next Tool asks you to consider both time and operational constraints—like how many of your metal sculptures will fit in the van you'll drive to county fairs, or how many antique cars you can store in your garage, or how much teak wood you can import from Indonesia. The constraint that holds you back the most sets the maximum number of customers you can serve. For example, if you have the time to serve 25 customers per month, but only have equipment capacity to serve 20, then you must evaluate the financial viability of your business based on 20 customers per month.

Let's go back to **Cheryl.** She has 120 worker hours available each month. She expects to spend four hours cleaning each house and anticipates that most clients will ask her to clean twice per month. She makes her calculations as follows: First, she divides 120 hours per month by the four hours that it will take her to clean each house. That means she can clean a total of 30 houses each month. But because she expects to clean each client's house twice per month, she divides her total in half, for a total of 15 clients that she has the capacity to serve.

CAPACITY TO SERVE YOUR CUSTOMERS

Step 1: Estimate your total capacity based on your time constraints.

Number of hours you plan to spend per month working on your business: ________(A)

Percentage of worker hours you plan to devote: ________(B)

Total hours you can use to serve customers (A x B): ________(C)

Estimated hours needed per customer: ________(D)

Total number of customers you can serve per month (C ÷ D): ________

Step 2: Estimate your total capacity based on your operational constraints.

My capacity is constrained by: ____________________

This constraint means I can only serve this many customers per month:

____

Step 3: Compare the number of customers you indicated in Steps 1 and 2 above. The lower number tells you the maximum number of customers you can serve each month.

Once you've competed the Tool above, compare your capacity to serve customers (Reality Check #2) to the number of customers needed to meet your financial goals (Reality Check #1). Do you have the capacity to serve the number of customers you need? If yes, you're ready to move on to the next reality check. If not, it's back to the drawing board. First, check your estimates and assumptions in the previous

Consider **Cheryl's** business one more time: She has determined that she can serve 15 customers per month. If her first reality check indicated that she needs 20 customers to meet her financial goals, she knows she has a problem. She must increase her capacity (perhaps by working more hours or hiring employees), reduce her costs, increase prices, or lower her financial goal. She can try various combinations of these strategies to see whether she can make her business work. If she can't, she'll have to rethink her business idea—it might not be the right business for her.

Tools. Make sure your calculations are reasonable. Evaluate your capacity limitations and determine whether there's another way to make your product or serve your customers. If you still show insufficient capacity to meet your goals, it means you need to go back to your Profile and consider a different business idea.

Reality Check #3: Can You Compete?

I don't know the key to success, but the key to failure is trying to please everybody.

—BILL COSBY

We've heard it hundreds of times from small business owners: "I have no competition." Well, that would be great—but it's almost never true. You will face competition. The question is whether you can achieve your financial and personal goals anyway. Can you successfully compete?

A potential customer will ask two questions when deciding whether they'll purchase the product or service you are offering:

- Will I buy this product or service from anyone?
- Will I buy it from this particular business?

The purpose of this section is to help you understand the factors that influence how potential customers answer these two questions. That will help you analyze your competition in Reality Check #3.

Will customers buy at all? Sometimes, business owners feel that they don't have any competition because they don't see other businesses that do the same thing. (This is called direct competition.) They look around town and don't see anyone else offering pink and purple dye jobs for pets, so they think they're in the clear. They forget that pet owners might decide to spend their money on something else.

Competition From Other Products and Services

Here are five reasons a potential customer may decide not to purchase your product or service at all (not from you or your direct competitors):

1. **Substitution.** In this circumstance, the customer buys a product that replaces or substitutes for your product. For example, a local pizza parlor could lose a sale because a potential customer decides to eat at a Mexican restaurant instead.
2. **Indirect competition.** Indirect competition comes from a business in another, but closely related, industry. A customer may decide not to eat at the pizza parlor or Mexican restaurant but, rather, buy a selection of prepared foods at a nearby grocery store.
3. **Do-it-yourselfers.** Do-it-yourselfers can be a significant form of competition for service businesses. They have a number of motivations for doing tasks themselves, such as saving money or enjoying the work required. Rather than eat at the pizza parlor, or any restaurant, a do-it-yourselfer will buy groceries and prepare meals at home.
4. **Buy something else.** Some potential customers may decide to spend their money seeing a movie and eating a box of popcorn.
5. **Do nothing.** These are potential customers who decide not to make a purchase at all. For the pizza parlor example, this could mean a potential customer decides not to eat dinner at all and go to bed early.

Understanding whether potential customers will buy products and services like yours will help you evaluate your potential for success. Recall the discussion in Chapter 8 about trends. It's hard to swim against the tide. For example, as the number of do-it-yourselfers has grown, so have the big box retailers—like Home Depot and Lowe's—that serve them. This might make it harder for a small business—such as a handyman or fence builder—to compete. It might still be possible, but you'll have to take all of your competition into account.

Remember the main question your customers will ask: "What's in it for me?" That will help you think about why they will buy your product or service instead of the many other things they could buy.

Will customers buy from your business? The second key question is whether customers will purchase from you or choose a competitor. You won't be establishing your business or targeting your customers in a vacuum. You'll most likely face direct competition, and to succeed you have to realistically evaluate strengths and weaknesses—both theirs and yours. This can help you turn competitors' weaknesses to your advantage, work to overcome your own weaknesses, and capitalize on your strengths. The following reality check will help you perform a competitive analysis to make sure you can keep your business a step ahead.

As mentioned, a direct competitor sells the same product or service as your business (the pizza parlors in the town where you live are all direct competitors with each other). Once they've decided to buy a product or service, customers choose to buy from a particular business for a variety of reasons, such as location, price, customer service, and reputation.

The following Tool asks you to look at your direct competitors. The Tool lists ten common competitive factors and has room for you to add others that are important in your situation. For each factor, assign a score to your business and each competitor. Use a scale from one to ten, with ten indicating a great strength and one indicating supreme weakness. You can give the same score to your business and one or more competitors if you think all are equal.

EVALUATING YOUR COMPETITION

Direct Competitor 1:______________________________

Direct Competitor 2:______________________________

Direct Competitor 3:______________________________

Competitive Factor	Your Business	Competitor 1	Competitor 2	Competitor 3
Quality				
Expertise				
Selection				
Reliability				
Customer Service				
Business Reputation				
Availability				
Sales Methods				
Payment Terms				
Price				
Other				

It appears the direct competition for this type of product/service is:

❑ Very strong—it will be hard to break in

❑ Moderate—they're good, but there's room for more

❑ Weak—there's great potential for my business

I believe I can successfully compete with these businesses: yes ❑ no ❑

Some of the competitive factors may be much more important to customers than others. A high score in such an area could mean a competitor is very strong, even if they score lower on other factors. Focus on how you feel about your chances for success against your competition. Later, when you actually start your business, you can use the Tool to help you emphasize your strengths and improve on your weaknesses.

After a long career as a school counselor, **Kerry** planned to retire and set up his own practice. He wanted to do this in the college town where his daughter and grandchildren lived. However, he learned there was an abundance of counselors in the town, many of whom were highly qualified and well-connected. Kerry concluded that the direct competition was very strong and it would be hard to break in. He changed his original idea and set up shop in a town 50 miles away—still close enough to his family but with much less competition.

What happens if it looks like your business idea can't compete? If there's too much strong competition to make your business idea work—especially given the time and money you wish to put into it—it's best to face that now. Although you shouldn't be afraid of competing (remember that there will always be competition), neither do you want to start a business if the competition is formidable. If that seems to be true, tweak your business idea or consider a different one.

Reality Check #4: Can You Finance Your Business Idea?

Unfortunately, some retirees never find out whether their great business idea would work—they lack the cash needed to open the doors. It can be very expensive to start a business. True, some businesses are more time-intensive than capital-intensive, but most still require some infusion of cash.

The Tools in this section will help you do the following:

- identify your start-up costs
- estimate your needed working capital (we'll define this in a moment), and
- calculate the cash you will need to open the doors of your business.

This will lead you to your final reality check: Do you have the money you need to get started or will you need to get more? And, how comfortable are you risking that much money on your business?

Start-Up Costs

You'll have to spend money to open your doors for business. These are your start-up costs—one time, up-front expenditures that you must handle before you begin. Start-up costs vary widely from business to business, but they may include the costs of equipment (capital expenditures), legal fees, licenses and permits, or even the expense of buying an existing business, if you don't start yours from scratch.

The next Tool helps you identify how much it will cost to start your business. Skip any costs that don't apply to your situation—but try to account for all of your up-front costs. For example, include any amounts you must pay to your landlord right away, perhaps first and last month's rent and a security deposit. If you'll be selling products, estimate what you must spend to get your first batch of products ready to sell (called your beginning inventory). Use your best estimate for each item, doing as much research as you need to get a reasonable dollar amount.

YOUR START-UP COSTS

Start-Up Cost	Dollar Amount
Beginning Inventory	
Capital Expenditures (equipment, computers, vehicles, furniture)	
Legal and Accounting Fees	
Public Utilities (hook-up charges, refundable deposits)	
Licenses and Permits	
Remodeling Work	
Rent (first month, security and cleaning deposits)	
Office Supplies	
Business Cards	
Advertising (brochures, flyers, posters)	
Website Design	
Payment to Former Owner or to Franchisor	
Other	
Total	

Working Capital

After you've started your business, you'll have to cover some expenses even if you haven't yet received cash from customers. For instance, you'll have to pay your cell phone bill, ongoing monthly rent, semiannual insurance premiums, and your suppliers. For all of these payments, you'll need what's called working capital.

Working capital is your cushion—the amount of cash you'll want to have on hand to pay bills and yourself. Businesses need working capital because cash from customers won't always arrive in time to pay the bills. Working capital bridges the gap. Most bankers recommend that you start a business with three or four months' working capital in the bank—and that you maintain at least two months' working capital at all times. When you start your business, you might need more working capital than that, depending on how long it takes for sales to kick in. The amount of working capital you'll need is, in part, a function of your attitude about risk. Here, the risk is that you'll run out of money, won't be able to pay your business bills on time, or won't bring in enough from the business to cover your personal expenses. If you're uncomfortable with risk, you'll want a bigger cushion than a risk taker would.

The next Tool helps you determine the amount of working capital you will need to pay yourself and your monthly fixed costs if you have no sales.

YOUR WORKING CAPITAL

Step 1: Estimate the number of months of cushion you'll need and enter it in Row A. You can do this twice: The first column covers the best case scenario (fewer months), and the second column addresses your worst case scenario (more months).

Step 2: Enter your monthly cash requirements in Row B for your best and worst cases. You can get this from "Customers Needed to Meet Financial Goals," Row C, above.

Step 3: Determine how much working capital you'll need.

	Best Case	**Worst Case**
(A) Number of Months		
(B) Monthly Cash Requirements		
(C) Working Capital Needed to Start Business = A x B		

You'll want to have working capital in some amount between your best and worse case scenarios. How much you decide to have should respect your attitude about risk. Choose a higher amount if you dislike the risk of running out of money or a lower amount if you're comfortable taking more risk.

Opening the Doors

You have determined your start-up costs and your working capital requirements. You'll need to finance both to open your business. For some people, the amounts are a shock, much more than they were thinking. The following Tool helps you answer two essential questions: Do you have enough money to start your business? If not, how much more will you need?

You can easily complete the Tool by referring to your Profile and the previous Tools in this chapter.

ABILITY TO FINANCE YOUR BUSINESS IDEA

Step 1: In Row A, enter the most you can invest and the amount you are comfortable investing to start your business (refer to your Profile for these amounts).

Step 2: Enter your total start-up costs in both columns.

Step 3: Enter your working capital in both columns.

Step 4: Calculate total cash needed to start your business.

Step 5: Determine any excess or shortfall.

	The Most I Can Invest to Start My Business	**How Much I Am Comfortable Investing in My Business**
(A) Amount of Investment		
(B) Start-Up Costs		
(C) Working Capital		
(D) Total Cash Needed to Start My Business = B + C		
(E) Excess or Shortfall = A – D		

Do you have the money you'll need to start your business? If not, then you'll need to raise some money or scale back your plans. Refer to your Profile and think about your attitude about money. If your chosen business idea requires more than you're comfortable investing, you may need to revisit your idea.

CROSS REFERENCE

If you'll need more money to start your business. If your reality check above shows that you'll need some extra cash to open your business, be sure to read Chapter 12 for information about tapping your own resources or borrowing from someone else.

Make Frequent Reality Checks

Ideas and projects often take on a life of their own. For example, your simple business idea, which was supposed to take only ten hours per week, could morph into a time-gobbling monster. Or, your plans to work by yourself may be altered by projects that require you to hire employees or take on a partner. Such changes might be just fine with you; your goals and desires will evolve over time. But you want to be sure that you're running your business rather than the other way around. Periodic testing of your chosen business idea using your Profile and the reality checks in this chapter is a great way to stay in touch with what you want from your retirement business.

Tony wanted to open an art gallery, specializing in fiber arts. She'd sell her own weavings and the knitted, woven, crocheted, and quilted products from many of her artist friends. But a problem arose when she estimated her start-up costs and working capital. It was way more than she wanted to invest in her business. It seemed the main reasons were the large amounts required for rent and remodeling to make the gallery the delightful place she wanted it to be. Tony explored other avenues and soon found she could sublet space in another gallery. The rent was much lower and the space needed very little work, so the costs fit with the amount Tony wanted to invest into her business.

Get Ready to Launch Your Business

Starting a retirement business is like being a kid in a neighborhood race. You walk up to the starting line and someone yells, "On your mark. Get set. Go!"

If you've completed the Tools in the earlier chapters of this book, you are already "on your mark." You've listed your retirement goals, inventoried your resources, chosen your business idea, and checked the reality of making it happen.

Now, it's time to "get set."

This step will help you get ready to start your business. We'll cover:

- **Legal issues**: like form of ownership, protecting your ideas, and contracts
- **Financing options**: including reverse mortgages and commercial loans, and how to write a business plan
- **Tax issues**: such as the self-employment tax and whether you'll have to pay taxes on your Social Security benefits
- **Health insurance**: including COBRA and Medicare
- **Finding help**: from attorneys, accountants, books, and websites.

It is beyond the scope of this book to discuss these topics in great depth, but we introduce the issues, help you keep track of tasks to accomplish, and provide resources for getting things done. For example, we'll introduce the different forms that your business may take—sole proprietorship, corporation, LLC, and so on—and then we'll direct you to the best sources for learning more about the particular business forms that interest you and for completing the necessary paperwork to get set up.

Once you've got a handle on the topics in this step, there's only one more thing to do: Go! Get out there and make it happen. Your successful retirement business is waiting for you.

CHAPTER

11

Handle Legal Matters

The minute you read something that you can't understand, you can almost be sure that it was drawn up by a lawyer.

—WILL ROGERS

A myriad of legal issues will influence the way you establish and operate your business. For example, will you be able to run your business as a relatively casual sole proprietorship or does your venture require the additional formalities and protections of a corporation? Will you need to register a business name—or a domain name if you want to have your own website? Are you ready to comply with zoning laws, employment regulations, or insurance requirements? Your legal setup will depend on the type of business you open, where you operate, and your personal financial and legal circumstances.

This chapter introduces the legal issues that are most important to small business owners. It will give you an overview of the rules that are likely to apply to you and help you make a list of the legal tasks you need to accomplish before you start your business. Be assured that you won't have to call an attorney every time you have a legal question. You can handle many basic legal matters on your own—and we point you toward resources that can help. And even if you do need a lawyer's help, knowing something about the issues will increase your comfort level and reduce your legal fees. (If you don't already know a good lawyer, you can learn more about finding one in Chapter 15.)

Keeping Track of Your Tasks

Whether you decide to handle legal matters yourself or seek help from a lawyer, it helps to keep track of your tasks and the decisions you make. The following Tool can help.

LEGAL TASKS AND DECISIONS

Topic	Tasks	Outcome/Decision
Form of Business Ownership	1. ______ 2. ______ 3. ______	Form chosen: ______
Business Name	1. ______ 2. ______ 3. ______	Name chosen: ______
Domain Name	1. ______ 2. ______ 3. ______	Domain name chosen: ______
Intellectual Property (IP)	1. ______ 2. ______ 3. ______	IP protected: ______
Noncompete Agreements	1. ______ 2. ______ 3. ______	Agreements signed by: ______
Business Location	1. ______ 2. ______ 3. ______	Location identified: ______
Business Leases	1. ______ 2. ______ 3. ______	Lease terms agreed upon: ______

LEGAL TASKS AND DECISIONS, continued

Topic	Tasks	Outcome/Decision
Local Regulations	1. ______ 2. ______ 3. ______	Regulations that apply: ______
Employees, Contractors, and Other Workers	1.______ 2.______ 3. ______	Help I plan to use: ______
Insurance and Bonds	1.______ 2.______ 3. ______	Types of coverage purchased: ______
Contracts	1.______ 2.______ 3. ______	Contracts drafted and signed: ______

As you read through the chapter, decide whether each of the legal matters discussed will apply to you and your business. If a topic doesn't apply, skip ahead. If there's an issue you need to take care of, keep track of what you need to do. For example, you might need to learn more about patents, register your business name, complete articles of incorporation, or have your lawyer review a contract. We've left space for three tasks per legal matter, but you can add additional tasks as needed.

The last column in the Tool gives you space to record your decisions and final outcomes for each legal matter.

Forms of Business Ownership

You must choose a form of ownership for your business. The possibilities include sole proprietorship, partnership, corporation, or limited liability company (LLC). Business owners generally use three main criteria when choosing their form of ownership: personal liability, income tax rules, and legal formalities.

- **Personal liability.** Under some forms of ownership, creditors can go after your personal assets to satisfy business debts. Other forms limit your personal liability—in other words, they protect your personal assets. This could be very important if you have lots of financial resources to shelter and are concerned about what might happen if your business doesn't succeed. Also, buying insurance to cover potential lawsuits can be unaffordable or unavailable—and it may be better to let your business carry the risk than to carry it personally. Of course there is a downside to this type of protection: You must follow strict documentation requirements in order to qualify for it and keep it.
- **Income taxes.** You must pay income tax on all of your business profits, but how that happens depends on your form of ownership. Either the business will pay income taxes separately or you will pay them personally. Sometimes, the methods are combined.
- **Legal formalities.** Some forms of ownership are simple to establish and easy to maintain. Others require a good deal of initial and ongoing paperwork. In all cases, financial information for the business must be kept separate from that of the owners. Failing to keep clear records can jeopardize the personal liability protection offered by some forms of ownership.

Sole Proprietorship

In a sole proprietorship, you are the only business owner, although some states allow your spouse to help out from time to time without being considered an owner or employee.

- **Personal liability.** You have unlimited personal liability. That means creditors can look to your personal property to satisfy business debts, if necessary.
- **Income taxes.** You report the business profit or loss on your personal income tax return. Because the business does not exist as an independent entity for tax purposes, it does not pay separate income taxes.
- **Legal formalities.** This is the simplest type of business to start and run. Generally, there are no legal documents required. That said, be sure to peruse the rest of this chapter for other laws that may apply to your business, such as those that will help you secure a business name or location.

Partnership

Partnerships have two or more owners. There are several types of partnership—the most common are general and limited partnerships.

- **Personal liability.** In a general partnership, all partners are personally liable for partnership obligations. Creditors can look to each partner to cover 100% of business debts. (In other words, the acts of just one partner could leave the others holding the bag. This means that you should go into business only with partners you completely trust.)
  A limited partnership has two types of partners: at least one general partner with unlimited personal liability, and limited partners whose liability is limited to their investment in the business.
- **Income taxes.** You report your share of the business profit or loss on your personal tax return. The business itself does not pay income taxes.
- **Legal formalities.** A partnership is usually formed by signing a partnership agreement. Among other things, the agreement usually covers each partner's share of profits and losses, day-to-day work duties, and what happens if a partner dies or retires. You can write an agreement yourself or seek help from a lawyer.

Corporation

A corporation is a legal entity owned by one or more people or other business entities, all of which are called shareholders. The corporation issues shares of stock in exchange for cash or other assets. Owners decide what amount of corporate profits to retain in the business and what amount to distribute to themselves as dividends.

The name of a corporation usually ends with "Incorporated" (Inc.) or "Limited" (Ltd.).

- **Personal liability.** Owner liability for corporate debts is limited to the amount invested in the business. Do note, however, that most lenders and some creditors require the owners of the business to personally guarantee corporate debts—this reduces personal liability protection.
- **Income taxes.** The business is a separate taxable entity that must prepare and file a corporate tax return. Generally, the business pays income taxes at rates that are lower than individual rates. However, each shareholder must pay taxes on any dividends received from the corporation. This means there is a danger of double taxation—once on the original profits and again on the dividends. The combined tax payments may be more than if you simply pay at your individual tax rate.
- **Legal formalities.** A corporation is formed by filing documents, usually called articles of incorporation, with your state's corporate filing office. The corporation must also establish bylaws (operating rules), conduct shareholder meetings, prepare minutes, and keep business finances strictly separate from those of shareholders. These legal formalities are often more than a small business owner wants to handle, so they choose to form a sole proprietorship or partnership instead.

What's an S Corporation?

An S corporation is like other corporations in all respects except how income taxes are paid. Unlike a regular corporation (also called a C corporation), an S corporation does not pay income tax itself. Instead, each shareholder reports their share of profit or loss on their personal tax return. An important advantage of this filing status is that shareholders can use corporate losses to offset personal income.

The disadvantages, however, are many. S corporations require additional paperwork and impose limitations on how owners may allocate business income and deduct expenses. Many business owners choose to form a limited liability company (LLC) instead. LLCs are discussed next.

Limited Liability Company (LLC)

An LLC is similar to a corporation in that is a legal entity separate from its owners. The owners of an LLC are called members. (An LLC can be formed with just one member.) The main difference between a corporation and an LLC is how the business is taxed.

- **Personal liability.** Members have limited personal liability for business debts. As with corporations, lenders and creditors may require the members to personally guarantee the debts of the LLC.
- **Income taxes.** The main benefit of an LLC is that it provides personal liability protection but lets you choose how to be taxed. An LLC may be taxed like a corporation, meaning that the business pays taxes on profits and members pay taxes on any salaries or distributions received. Or, an LLC may be taxed like a sole proprietorship or partnership, in which case the business pays no income taxes and you account for the profit or loss on your personal tax return.
- **Legal formalities.** To form an LLC, you must file a document, usually called articles of organization, with your state's corporate filing office. Ongoing legal requirements differ from state to state, but they are generally less burdensome than those for a corporation.

RESOURCE

Resources to help you choose the right form for your business. You can easily find a wealth of information to help you select and set up the best form for your business. We recommend that you begin with the free articles available on Nolo's website at www.nolo.com. For more details, you can turn to one or more of the following publications.

Getting an Overview

Legal Guide for Starting & Running a Small Business, by Fred S. Steingold (Nolo), explains what you need to know to choose the right form for your business and shows you what to do to get it started.

The Small Business Start-Up Kit, by Peri H. Pakroo (Nolo), shows you how to choose from among the basic types of business organizations, file the right forms, get the proper licenses and permits, and handle basic record keeping.

Sole Proprietorships

Working for Yourself: Law & Taxes for Independent Contractors, Freelancers & Consultants, by Stephen Fishman (Nolo), is an excellent resource for those who are self-employed and offering their services on a contract basis—as do many sole proprietors. It shows independent contractors how to meet business start-up requirements, comply with IRS rules, and make sure they get paid in full and on time.

Small Time Operator, by Bernard Kamoroff, C.P.A. (Bell Springs Publishing), is a good source of practical information on getting a sole proprietorship off the ground—from securing a business license, to paying taxes, to handling basic accounting. It includes ledgers and worksheets to get you started.

Partnerships

Form a Partnership: The Complete Legal Guide, by Ralph Warner and Denis Clifford (Nolo), explains the legal and practical issues involved in forming a business partnership, creating a partnership agreement, and protecting each person's interests.

Corporations

Incorporate Your Business: A Legal Guide to Forming a Corporation in Your State, by Anthony Mancuso (Nolo), shows you how to set up and run a corporation in any state.

LLCs

LLC or Corporation? How to Choose the Right Form for Your Business, by Anthony Mancuso (Nolo), provides all the details to help you decide whether an LLC or a corporation is better for your business.

Form Your Own Limited Liability Company, by Anthony Mancuso (Nolo), explains how to set up an LLC in any state, without hiring a lawyer.

Protecting Creative Ideas

You may have a clever business name, an invention, a new process or an innovative concept that will be your key to success. You need to protect your creative ideas from unauthorized use. This section shows you where to start.

Business Name

Your first step in securing a business name depends on whether you plan to operate as a sole proprietor or whether you will form a corporation or LLC.

If you plan to incorporate or form an LLC, the formal name of your business is set when you file your formation documents with the state. For example, your articles of incorporation may be for ABC, Inc. Start by checking with the Secretary of State's office in your state to be sure that your proposed name isn't the same or confusingly similar to an existing corporate or LLC name. You'll need to choose a name that's distinct from everyone else's.

You may conduct business using this name or you may use an assumed business name, commonly referred to as a DBA (doing business as). ABC, Inc. doesn't say much about what your company does, so you may decide to do business as Cascade Fishing Lures. Sole proprietors may operate using an assumed business name, too.

If you want to use an assumed business name, check with your county clerk or Secretary of State to see whether the name you want to use is already on the list of fictitious or assumed business names. (In most locations, fictitious or assumed business names are maintained by the county. The state handles them in only a handful of places.) If your chosen name is available, follow the instructions on how to register it.

Naming Your Business

Here are some considerations in designing your business name:

- Does it tell what your business does?
- Is it easy to remember, pronounce, and spell? Don't pick a name that's too bland to remember or too long to be comfortably spoken or written.
- Is it too easily confused with the name of a competitor or a nationally known company? Even if your chosen name isn't listed with your county or state, you won't want to step on the toes of a national company's trademark or servicemark rights. (For more information, see "Intellectual Property," below.)
- Do you like the name? After all, you're the person who's going to hear it and say it the most.
- Should the business name be your name? This can be especially effective for service businesses.

Domain Name

Do you plan to have a website for your business? Even a simple one-page Web presence can be useful. Every website has a unique address, usually called a domain name. You can protect your domain name by registering it online. You can register as many domain names as you wish.

Keep in mind that many domain names have already been snapped up. Choosing a domain name that contains all or part of your business name will make it easier for potential customers to find your website. You might want to check to see what's available before you settle on a name for your business.

RESOURCE

Get your domain name. There are a number of websites where you can check availability and register your domain name. Some popular websites are:

- www.register.com
- www.godaddy.com
- www.networksolutions.com.

Choosing a Domain Name

Here are some things to think about when choosing your domain name:

- Does the name convey what your company does—or is it too generic? (Remember, it's often a good idea to secure a domain name that includes your business name.)
- Is it easy to remember or is it too tricky? You'll usually want to avoid odd spellings or symbols.
- Is it too long? Internet users are impatient.
- Is the name too cute? Very clever puns or hip phrases can confuse customers and they may appear unprofessional.
- Is it too easily confused with another domain name?
- Have you tried conjoining words? Even though long, these names often do a great job of conveying what you do and are easy to remember—for example, www.booksforteens.com.

Intellectual Property

Copyrights, trademarks, and patents are used to protect intellectual property. They are regulated by the federal government.

- **Copyrights.** Copyrights are used to protect original artistic creations, including songs, movies, books, newspaper and magazine articles, pictures, and computer software. Under federal law, copyright protection exists the moment a protected work is created. It is not legally necessary to include a copyright notice on the work but, practically speaking, it's always a good idea. A copyright notice prevents others from claiming they didn't know that your work was protected. A valid copyright notice contains the word "copyright," the copyright symbol (a "c" in a circle), the name of the author or the owner of the copyright rights, and the date of publication—for example, Copyright © 2008 by David Johnson. In addition, you can strengthen your rights by registering your creative work with the U.S. Copyright Office (www.copyright.gov). Most copyrights are good for the life of the creator plus 70 years.
- **Trademarks and servicemarks.** Trademarks protect words, slogans, symbols, or other devices that distinguish the goods of one company from another. Think of the "swoosh" used by Nike or the name Walkman used by Sony. A servicemark is similar to a trademark, except it promotes a service or event rather than a product. Consider the Olympic Games' multicolored interlocking circles, which promote an international sporting event, or the name FedEx Kinko's, which identifies a photocopying service. You claim ownership of a trademark or servicemark by being the first to use it in the marketplace. You can also protect a trademark by registering the mark with the U.S. Patent and Trademark Office (www.uspto.gov) before anyone else uses it. Many businesses put a "TM" or "SM" symbol next to their mark to indicate that they own it, but it's not legally necessary to do so. However, an "R" in a circle (®) is a different animal—it may not be used unless a mark has been registered with the federal government. Trademarks and servicemarks last as long as you continue to use them.

- **Patents.** A patent gives you the right to exclude others from making, using, offering for sale, selling, or importing your invention. The U.S. Patent and Trademark Office (www.uspto.gov) puts forth detailed rules about the types of inventions that do or do not qualify for protection. If you've got an invention you want to protect, you'll need to do some careful research to be sure it meets the rigorous standards. If your invention qualifies, you can apply to the PTO for a patent. A patent provides great legal protection for inventions but the application process can be very long and expensive. Most patents are good for 20 years.

RESOURCE

Help with copyrights, trademarks, and patents. For more information about copyright, trademarks, and patents, visit Nolo's website at www.nolo.com. You'll find free, detailed articles on a variety of intellectual property topics. For more, you can turn to the following Nolo publications:

The Copyright Handbook: What Every Writer Needs to Know, by Stephen Fishman. This book is a complete guide to copyright rules. It includes forms for registering your copyrights.

Trademark: Legal Care for Your Business & Product Name, by Stephen Elias. This guide shows you how to choose a legally strong business and product name, register the name with state and federal agencies, and handle trademark disputes.

Nolo's Patents for Beginners, by David Pressman and Richard Stim. This book provides a thorough overview of what it takes to obtain a patent, including an explanation of how to prepare and file a provisional patent application.

Patent It Yourself, by David Pressman. The ultimate guide to patent protection, this book takes you step by step through the process of getting a patent without hiring a patent lawyer.

Noncompete Agreements

If you plan to hire employees or buy a business, or if someday you decide to sell your business, you might need to sign a noncompete agreement.

This type of agreement prohibits someone from working for a direct competitor or opening a competing business, in your market area for a specified length of time. The agreement also prevents the other person from using or disclosing confidential information and trade secrets. To learn more, visit Nolo's website at www.nolo.com.

Your Business Location

When it comes to location, there are two main legal issues you should investigate: zoning regulations and leases. As a first rule, don't sign a lease until you're 100% certain that you will be allowed to operate your business in that location. Begin by researching the local rules and regulations that may affect your business.

Zoning Regulations

Cities and counties regulate what type of businesses, if any, can operate in various locations. No matter where you'll operate—from home or an outside office, store, or shop—you must comply with zoning regulations. Permission from your landlord is not enough.

In addition, local governments may impose other regulations covering matters such as parking, signs, noise, lighting, fire regulations, and handicapped access. Failure to comply can cause difficulties with neighbors and carry hefty penalties and fines.

If your city has a business development office, it can help you understand and address all of these restrictions. Your local Chamber of Commerce, economic development organization, or Small Business Development Center are other sources of information about local regulations.

Keep in mind, too, that your business may come up against some private rules. For example, if you want to locate your business in a mall, you'll want to talk with management about what you're allowed to do there. Shopping complexes may place limits on the numbers or types of businesses that can operate on the premises.

Leases

Very few new businesses purchase property. Instead, they lease space. Because you're just starting out and may be unsure of your space needs (and ability to pay the rent), you might be inclined to rent on a month-to-month basis, which allows you to move with little notice. Unfortunately, it's uncommon to find landlords willing to fix-up and rent space for less than a period of years (two to five is a common minimum amount). But take heart—though you lose some flexibility with a lease of a few years, you'll have the assurance that the space is yours for enough time to give your new venture a fighting start. And knowing what your rent obligations will be for the foreseeable future will allow you to factor in a set amount for rent as you develop your business idea.

The lease will specify several key terms of the deal, including the start date, permissible use of the space, parking, deposits, and most importantly, the rent. Small retail businesses typically rent by the square foot (be sure to confirm the landlord's measurements with your own). You may also be asked to pitch in on common area maintenance costs (upkeep of lobbies, stairs, corridors, and parking lots) if you rent in a building with other tenants; and you may be asked to contribute to the landlord's tax and insurance costs.

Questions to Ask About Leases

If you will be leasing property, here are some questions you might wish to ask during negotiations:

- What exactly am I leasing? How is square footage calculated?
- Does the lease have a renewal option? If so, what are the terms?
- Are there scheduled rent increases? How are they calculated?
- Who pays for and owns any improvements made to the property?
- Are certain business activities prohibited?
- Am I able to sublet or assign the lease?
- What happens if the lessor decides to sell the property?

RESOURCE

Help with leases. Before you sign a lease, learn all you can with *Negotiate the Best Lease for Your Business,* by Janet Portman and Fred Steingold (Nolo). It gives you all the information you need to choose the right spot and negotiate a commercial lease.

Employees vs. Independent Contractors

Even if you plan to operate your business mostly by yourself, it's still likely that you'll need some help from time to time. If free help from your spouse or grandchildren just won't do, you have three choices: Hire an employee, engage an independent contractor, or use an agency that provides temporary workers.

If you'll be hiring workers, it's important to know the legal difference between an employee and an independent contractor. An employee is someone who works for a company or organization under its direction and control. An independent contractor, on the other hand, performs work under his or her own direction and control. The distinction is very important. Having an employee brings into play federal, state, and local employment laws. These laws do not apply to independent contractors.

It's expensive and time consuming to comply with employment laws, so businesses have tried many schemes to call their workers independent contractors instead. Of course federal and state agencies are wise to this game, and they lean hard on business owners who are a little too creative when defining the status of their workers.

Unfortunately, there's not just one standard for determining whether a worker is an employee or an independent contractor. Different agencies use different tests—for example, the IRS looks at the question one way, while state workers' compensation boards take a different approach. But the analysis often turns on questions such as the following:

- **Who is in charge of how the work gets done?** With an employee, the business owner has the right to control what is done and how it's done. With an independent contractor, the business owner controls the end result but not how the work gets done.
- **Who bears the risk of loss?** Typically, an employee is reimbursed for expenses and invests no money in the business. On the other hand, an independent contractor usually makes a significant business investment, incurs expenses, and realizes profits and losses.
- **Does the worker get benefits?** Independent contractors usually work without benefits, under written agreements.

If you pay someone as an independent contractor and a government agency later finds that person to be an employee, it will cost you dearly. You'll have to pay the federal and state taxes that would otherwise have been paid, plus penalties and interest.

RESOURCE

Help for employers. You can find free legal articles for employers on Nolo's website at www.nolo.com. In addition, the following Nolo books will help you hire and manage employees or independent contractors:

The Employer's Legal Handbook, by Fred Steingold, explains employers' legal rights and responsibilities in detail.

Working With Independent Contractors, by Stephen Fishman, shows you how to determine who qualifies as an independent contractor, create valid contracts, and more.

Insurance and Bonding

You're going to take on some risks when you start your business. Some of these risks—like losing a big sale, facing increased expenses, or dealing with a new competitor—you'll just have to shoulder. But you can shift the burden for some risks by buying insurance.

Some states dictate the types of insurance a business must have, but most insurance coverage is optional. Small business owners commonly carry one or more of the following types of insurance.

- **Liability insurance** provides coverage if you or one of your employees accidentally injures someone or damages their property. The cost depends on the specific risks of your business.
- **Property insurance** covers your business's real estate, equipment, and other property. Policies generally protect against losses from theft, fire, and vandalism. Be sure to ask if you're also covered for floods, windstorms, hail damage, explosions, terrorism, and other catastrophes. If you'll be operating from home, ask your insurance agent what is covered by your homeowner's insurance policy. You may not need additional coverage. If you are renting space, make sure you understand what your landlord covers and what falls to you.
- **Commercial automobile insurance** is like insurance on your personal vehicle but covers vehicles used in the business. Think about carrying higher liability limits than you do on your personal car.
- **Business interruption insurance** covers loss of income if your business must close due to an event listed in the policy, such as a fire or earthquake. This type of insurance is generally used by businesses with high risks of losses from covered events, such as restaurants, which face a higher risk of fire than most businesses.
- **Errors and omissions insurance,** often called malpractice insurance, covers liability for negligent acts, errors, and omissions committed by professionals, including physicians, accountants, and lawyers. For example, real estate brokers typically carry this coverage in case they give faulty advice or mislead buyers and sellers about property conditions.
- **Product liability insurance** covers claims of harm caused by defective products. Most people associate faulty products with big companies, such as those that make the toxic toys and exploding gasoline engines we see on the evening news. But be aware that products of small businesses can fail, too. If you'll be selling products with the potential to harm people or property (like food, chemical products, or anything

that runs on electricity), you'll want to check with your insurance professional about whether product liability insurance is right for you.

To make sure you're covered for the risks unique to your business, consult an insurance agent who specializes in business insurance. If you decide not to purchase insurance, be sure to understand the potential consequences. If you feel you can't afford insurance, you need to ask yourself whether you can afford to be in business.

CROSS REFERENCE

Health insurance. Health care coverage is so important to most retirees that we've devoted an entire chapter to it. See Chapter 14.

Contracts

A verbal contract isn't worth the paper it's written on.

—SAMUEL GOLDWYN

As you conduct business, you're going to make deals with customers, employees, suppliers, your banker, your landlord—just about everyone you do business with. You'll agree to perform services, or lease space, or pay back a loan. Some of these agreements will constitute contracts that give you and the other party legal rights if something goes wrong. A legal contract contains the following four elements:

- **Agreement.** You and the other party must agree on the terms of the contract, often referred to as having a meeting of the minds. This results when one party makes an offer and the other party accepts. For example, you may offer to repair your customer's garage door opener, charging $70 per hour. If the customer accepts, you have an agreement.

- **Consideration.** You must exchange things of value. These can be services, cash, products, or other tangible items—or a promise to give one of these. Going back to our example above: If you have promised to fix the garage door opener and your customer has promised to pay you, you have exchanged things of value (promises).
- **Capacity.** All parties must be mentally capable of entering into the contract. People who may not be allowed to make a valid contract include minors, those who suffer from mental illness, or anyone under the influence of drugs or alcohol.
- **Legality.** You generally can't enforce a contract involving illegal activities. And some contracts must be in writing to be valid.

Unless a contract falls into one of the categories listed below, it is binding even if you don't write anything down. That said, you should put all of your important contracts in writing. If they're not, any disputes will be much more difficult to resolve. So by all means, shake hands on the deal, but remember to document the details and sign what you've written.

Written Agreements

State laws often require the following types of contracts to be written and signed by all parties:

- Contracts involving the sale of real estate or an interest in real estate.
- Lease of real estate for more than one year.
- Lease of personal property, such as equipment, for more than one year.
- Contract for services that will take more than one year to perform.
- A promise to pay the debt of another person.
- Contract to sell tangible items worth $500 or more.

Before You Sign

- Read the entire contract. The fine print is important.
- Be clear about exactly what you must do to satisfy your part of the agreement.
- Know what happens if either party fails to keep their promises under the contract.
- Decide whether you need an attorney to review the contract. Think about how you deal with risk and weigh that with the amount of money the contract involves and how important it is for the success of your business. The more at stake, the more likely it is that you'll want some professional advice.

RESOURCE

More information about business contracts. You can find a thorough discussion of business contracts in the *Legal Guide for Starting & Running a Small Business*, by Fred Steingold (Nolo).

CHAPTER

12

Finance Your Business

In all realms of life it takes courage to stretch your limits, express your power, and fulfill your potential … it's no different in the financial realm.
—SUZE ORMAN

When you come right down to it, there are only two possible sources of financing for your business: you or someone else. Most common, by far, is for small business owners to fund their own ventures. Most small businesses begin with only the owner's money on the line—this is especially true for home-based businesses.

Funding your own business doesn't just mean taking money from savings accounts and investments. There are other sources of personal financing for you to consider, including home equity loans, borrowing from your 401(k) plan, and reverse mortgages. If you need money for your business, personal resources might be the first place to look.

But your own money may not be enough. You might be opening a business precisely because you lack the resources to do the things you need and want to do. In that case, you'll have to raise money from someone else. And make no mistake about it—raising money is hard work, especially for new businesses. You'll have to convince someone that you and your business idea are worth the risk. You can do it; it's just a matter of learning how.

The good news is that you've already taken the first step toward financing your business, whether using your money or someone else's, by calculating your start-up costs, working capital, and financing needs in Chapter 10. Take some time to review your calculations and update them if you have better information now.

As you think about financing, you should also consider your feelings about risk. Look back at your work in Chapter 2 where you explored your attitudes about money. If you are very cautious, you're likely to invest or borrow less than someone who is more of a risk taker.

In this chapter, we introduce both personal and outside sources of financing. The amount of money you need and how much you're willing to risk will determine how you put these sources to work for you—one or more of the ideas below might be right for your business. We also introduce the basics of writing a business plan, something you'll need to do if you plan to get money from someone else.

We've included a Tool at the end of the chapter to help you summarize your financing plan—both how much money you'll need and how you will get it.

Not Too Little, Not Too Much

Many small businesses start on a shoestring. That's just fine unless the string is too short. Starting without enough money (being under-capitalized) can lead to a vicious cycle of cash flow troubles. If you don't have enough money to pay your rent or replenish supplies, you'll have a hard time staying in business. In a survey conducted by the National Federation of Independent Businesses, 67% of business owners said they have at least occasional problems managing cash flow, and 19% reported that cash flow is a continuing problem. You want to be part of the other 81%.

On the other hand, some business owners spend far too much money establishing their business. This, too, can lead to trouble.

As you establish your business, try to strike a balance. Ask yourself whether the costs you're anticipating are really necessary to get your business off the ground, but don't shortchange your business. Keep your customers in mind and their question of "What's in it for me?" Spending money to solve their problems and fulfill their desires is probably a good use of resources.

Maggie had a dream: soft candlelight, fine linens, savory smells of garlic and herbs, romantic dinners served by white-coated waiters in a Tuscan ambiance. She opened just such a restaurant in the small town where she lived, but her dream business was doomed from the start. Everything needed to be just so, a perfect portrayal of her dream. Marble floors, custom-built wine racks, top-of-the-line stoves, everything first class. It was far too expensive. The restaurant could not produce enough cash flow to cover the loans for the initial start-up costs and continuing overhead. It closed after only six months.

Using Your Own Money

Have you considered all possible sources of personal financing? Most likely, you've focused on using money you have in savings accounts, stocks, and mutual funds. But you may have additional resources to consider.

- **Take out a home equity loan.** Your home may be the most valuable asset you own and a good source of financing. You can either take out a second mortgage on your home, refinance the mortgage you already have, or negotiate a home equity line of credit. Home equity loans often involve monthly payments that begin right away, so be sure to figure these payments into your financial plans.
- **Use a reverse mortgage.** A reverse mortgage (generally available if you are at least 62 years old) lets you borrow against the equity in your home without having to make monthly payments. The loan is repaid when you die, sell your home, or move out permanently. These mortgages work in reverse of traditional mortgages, in that the debt balance increases rather than decreases over time. That means a high debt balance and low homeowner equity in the end. In essence, you are spending your equity over the years rather than watching it build. This can be a good financial strategy, especially if you are not concerned with the value of your estate. However, reverse mortgages are dangerous if the loan proceeds are spent carelessly. You wouldn't want to end up needing cash but have no equity in your home to borrow against.
- **Borrow from your 401(k) plan.** If you have a 401(k) plan (a tax-deferred savings account plan sponsored by an employer), you may be able to withdraw money from it. But there are very stringent rules about how and when you may do this, and penalties may apply if you aren't careful. If you aren't yet eligible to withdraw from your plan, or want to leave most of your money in your account, earning tax-free income, it might be better to borrow from your 401(k) instead. This can carry some steep fees and involve some paperwork. Each plan is different, so check with your plan administrator about limits, fees, and legal requirements. And do remember that until you repay the

loan, you're foregoing the tax-free income those dollars would have earned in your 401(k).

- **Borrow against insurance policies.** If you own whole-life insurance policies (these give you life insurance for your entire life, rather than just for a set number of years), check with your insurance agent about the possibility of borrowing against the cash value. As long as you pay the premiums, insurance companies are usually willing to lend a high percentage of the cash value while keeping the insurance benefit intact. Any unpaid loan amount will reduce benefits paid at death. Both the interest rates and the process can be quite reasonable.
- **Borrow against a certificate of deposit (CD).** Penalties can make it very expensive to pull money out of certificates of deposit before they come due. Instead, you might be able to borrow money using your CD as collateral. This arrangement often involves monthly loan interest payments and has no effect on the CD balance as long as the loan is repaid in full on a timely basis. Talk to the financial institution that holds your CD about this arrangement.

If you use your personal assets to fund your business, do recognize the potential impact on your retirement finances. You'll be reducing your financial resources unless your business earns enough to pay back what you put into it.

SKIP AHEAD

If you'll use only personal sources of financing. If you won't need outside sources of financing, you can skip to the discussion of business plans at the end of this chapter.

Getting Money From Others

When raising money, businesses have two basic choices: borrowing money outright or giving up an ownership share of the business (equity). Very few retirees raise money by taking on additional business owners, so our discussion focuses on borrowing.

Anyone lending you money expects two things in return: to get their money (the loan principal) back some day and to earn interest. Lenders generally want you to start making payments right away, although some lenders are willing to wait for their money until your business is well-established. In either case, borrowing money means that some of the cash flowing into your business must go to lenders rather than into your own pocket. Your business must generate enough cash to cover these debt payments and still provide you the income you're counting on. If selling to 30 customers was enough to provide for your personal needs, you may now need 40 customers.

Following are a number of loan sources you may want to consider.

Friends and Family

Most would-be business owners who need to borrow money look first to their friends and family. This can work well if your relationships are strong. Ideally, these people trust you, will be excited about your business, and want you to succeed. They might even be satisfied with a lower interest rate on their loan than a bank would charge.

However, there are potential problems with borrowing from those close to you, especially if your business fails. If you have to tell your brother that you've lost his savings, how will you feel, and how will he react? The many uncertainties involved in starting a business mean that it's important to keep your loan arrangements as businesslike as possible. Prepare a written loan agreement, specifying at least the amount of the loan, any interest due, when you'll make payments, and how much those payments will be. Make sure those who agree to help you understand the risks involved in your business. Keep them up-to-date on your successes and failures.

Also, be clear that the cash is a loan, not equity financing. If your brother thinks he is buying into your business, he might start hanging around, offering lots of advice. If that's what you want, by all means, take him on as a partner. But if you want to be independent, make sure everyone understands the limits of the relationship.

RESOURCE

More information about raising money from friends and family. *Investors in Your Backyard*, by Asheesh Advani (Nolo), provides information, forms, and financial calculators to help you raise business capital from people you already know—friends, family, or other private investors who believe in your business ideas.

Commercial Bank Term Loans

Commercial banks most often lend money to small businesses on a short-term basis–for example, 90 or 120 days. You need to be very confident that you can generate enough cash to repay the loan when it comes due. Interest rates are usually fixed, though payment arrangements vary. Some lenders will require monthly payments while others will want you to pay the entire principal balance plus interest on the date the loan is due.

If you want a long-term loan from a commercial bank, you may be able to get one, but you'll probably have to guarantee the loan either with assets from your business or with your personal assets. (If you default on the loan, the bank gets your property.) These loans usually require monthly installment payments.

Match Your Loan Term to Your Needs

In the world of finance, it's often said that short-term loans suit short-term needs and long-term borrowing should be reserved for projects that will take some time. Following this rule can help you generate enough cash to meet your loan obligations. As an example, let's say you borrow $40,000 to buy a piece of equipment. You wouldn't want a 90-day loan, because it's unlikely that equipment will help you generate enough cash to pay back the $40,000, plus interest, in so short a time. Perhaps a three-year term would be more appropriate. Likewise, it would be unwise to use a long-term loan to finance the purchase of inventory because those goods will be long gone even as you continue to make payments on the loan.

Line of Credit

You may be able to obtain a line of credit from a bank or credit union. These loans allow you to borrow just as much as you need up to a preapproved limit. You can repay the loan in full as soon as funds are available or establish a monthly repayment schedule. A line of credit is intended to be a short-term loan, typically used to get a business through a seasonal money crunch or bridge the gap until customer payments are received. Because of initial fees and variable interest rates, a line of credit usually is not suited for covering business start-up costs unless you're very confident you'll make enough money in your business to repay the loan quickly.

Credit Cards

Some new business owners rely on credit cards to finance their business. This can be a good strategy for meeting short-term cash needs—for example, if you need to purchase a computer or two—but be very careful. Interest rates on credit cards can be exorbitant. Also, it can be very difficult to monitor balances if you have lots of credit cards. If you're late with a payment on one card, it just might trigger higher interest rates on others.

If you think you'll be using credit cards to cover major purchases for your business, now would be a good time to do some research to make sure your cards carry the most favorable possible terms. If your record is good, it may take no more than a phone call to get a credit card company to lower your interest rate.

Leasing

A recent survey indicated that more than 70% of small businesses lease some of their assets. Under a lease, you (the lessee) are renting equipment or buildings from the owner (the lessor) rather than buying them. This can significantly reduce the amount of money you need to start your business because most leases require little, if any, up front payment.

A lease may be easier to obtain than a commercial bank loan. The lessor owns the asset, so will be less worried about what happens if you fail to make payments. Also, lease financing can be arranged with a bank, equipment manufacturer, landlord, or leasing company. You'll have more potential financers than if you deal only with commercial banks, so you can shop around for the best terms.

You can usually negotiate the length of a lease to suit your needs. A longer lease term allows you to stretch your payments out, while a shorter term allows you to more easily change locations or switch to new technology. Of course, a short lease term means you will soon be negotiating a new lease, putting you at risk for price increases.

The downside of leasing is that your total lease payments will exceed the cost of buying the equipment or building outright. You don't want to pay an exorbitant amount on a lease, so be sure you understand the numbers.

CROSS REFERENCE

More about the legal side of leases. If you think your business will lease property, be sure to read the discussion in Chapter 11 about the legal issues involved.

Customers

Your customers may be a wonderful source of financing. The idea is to collect money up front so you can cover your business costs until the remaining payments are received. If yours is a service business, you can negotiate retainers, advances, or progress payments. For example, family counselors may collect for visits in advance—or a portrait artist may require half of the total price upon starting a painting.

For product businesses, you can require down payments or payment in full upon ordering. For instance, interior decorators often require up front payment for all custom materials to be ordered.

Suppliers

If your business will sell products, ask your suppliers for credit terms on purchases. Having 30 days to pay, rather than paying when the goods are delivered, can reduce the amount of money you need to open your business. This type of supplier financing is usually interest-free.

As a new business, it may be difficult to convince suppliers to extend credit, but do try. Get to know the supplier representatives personally. Talk on the phone or, if possible, in person, so they have a voice or face to go with your business name. Pay on time, keep in contact, and establish a professional business relationship.

Government and Nonprofit Assistance

You might qualify for help from government or nonprofit organizations, such as the Small Business Administration (SBA), a Certified Development Corporation (CDC), or a Microloan Program. These organizations generally have economic development goals—for example, support of disadvantaged business owners or employment growth.

Don't fall into the trap of thinking that the government hands out money for free. Most government assistance programs are for loans or loan guarantees, not grants. Despite what some advertisements claim, free government money rarely exists. However, a number of programs do ease access to capital for small businesses. It's not easy to get this type of financing—eligibility requirements are strict—but it could be worth a try.

SBA Loan Guarantees

The SBA does not make loans directly to businesses. Instead, it guarantees loans made by commercial banks (discussed above) and other organizations described in this section. If a borrower does not repay the lender, the SBA steps in to cover the loan. Since this significantly reduces the lender's risk, an SBA guarantee can make the difference between denial and approval of your loan request.

The most common SBA loan program is called the SBA Guaranteed Loan Program or 7(a) Loan Guaranty Program. Both the lender and an SBA representative will very carefully review your business plan (more about that at the end of this chapter) and judge your potential for success.

Certified Development Corporations

A CDC is a private, nonprofit corporation established to encourage economic development in a particular community or region. These corporations administer the SBA 504 Program, which provides loans made jointly by a private lender and the CDC. The CDC's portion of the loan is guaranteed by the SBA. The funds are generally used to finance real estate or equipment acquisition.

Microloans

Microloans—never more than $35,000—are targeted at new businesses and made to finance the purchase of inventory, supplies, furniture, or equipment. Microloan programs are administered by nonprofit community-based organizations, often the local Certified Development Corporation.

State and Local Assistance

There may be many loan programs available from your state and local governments. These may be loan guarantee programs, direct loans, or loans made through lending intermediaries, like banks and credit unions. Your state may even have some limited grant programs.

RESOURCE

More information about government loan programs. To learn about all available Small Business Administration loan and guarantee programs, visit the SBA website at www.sba.gov/financing. To check out state and local assistance programs, contact the nearest Small Business Development Center (SBDC). (You can learn more about SBDCs in Chapter 15.)

Working With a Lender

If you would know the value of money, try to borrow some.

—BENJAMIN FRANKLIN

Before anyone will lend you money, you'll have to convince them that it's in their best interest. Banks and credit unions make loans using other people's money, so they'll be cautious. To get a loan, it helps to understand where your lender is coming from, anticipate his or her concerns, and address those up front.

Know the Five Cs of Credit

If you're applying for a loan from a financial institution, your loan officer will consider the Five Cs of Credit. Even if you're asking someone you know for money, it's wise to think carefully about these points. Your friends, family, or other supporters will want to know what they're getting into.

Here, we introduce each concern. In the next section, we'll give you some tips for addressing them when you meet with a lender.

- **Conditions.** Is your business in a growing industry or a dying one? Do market conditions support your cash flow projections?
- **Character.** Are you trustworthy, determined, and hardworking? Do you have what it takes to make this business work?
- **Collateral.** What can you pledge as collateral for the loan? Collateral is an asset, like equipment or real estate, that secures the loan. If you fail to make payments, the lender takes ownership of the collateral. Financial institutions usually want the value of the collateral to exceed the loan amount. Your new business probably won't have much to offer as collateral, so the lender may ask for some of your personal assets as collateral. If you will establish your business as a corporation or LLC, be aware that this might negate some of your liability protection.

- **Capital.** How much money will you invest in your business? Most lenders want you to have plenty at stake before they'll join in. They know that if your own money is on the line, you'll probably work harder and smarter on your business. On average, lenders expect your investment to be at least 20%–25% of the total business needs.
- **Capacity.** Will you be able to make your loan payments? A lender wants to be reasonably confident that your business will generate enough cash to pay loan principal and interest on time. Your lender will judge this by reviewing your credit history, sales forecast, and cash flow projection.

Be Prepared

Getting a loan isn't easy but you can make the whole process smoother and increase your chances for success if you're well prepared. Here are some tips on getting your loan request approved:

Write a business plan. Keep the Five Cs of Credit in mind. Make sure your plan is neat, understandable, and mathematically correct. (For more about business plans, see "Writing a Business Plan," below.)

Create a cover letter. Your letter should include the purpose of the loan, the amount of money you need, the length of the loan you want, information about how you will repay the loan, and any collateral that is available to secure the funds.

Get to know your lender before you need a loan. Remember "character" in the Five Cs—your lender will have a head start on this factor if he or she knows you.

Make an appointment. Don't just drop in. This will demonstrate respect for your lender. The lender will appreciate the courtesy and be more likely to make time for you in their schedule.

Sell your business idea first. If a lender is excited about your business, they're more likely to approve your loan request. Take the time to convince them that you've got a great idea and that you can make it a success. Ask about the loan and terms only after you've convinced your lender that you and your business are a good investment.

Your Credit History and Score

Lenders are putting more emphasis on credit history than ever before. That's because advances in technology have made it easy for them to get your credit history and credit score, which are more objective measures of risk than your character or current market conditions. Some financial institutions now even use impersonal, online loan applications and no longer evaluate the Five Cs for small loans.

If you'll be applying for loans, this is a good time to review your credit history and clean up any errors. You're entitled to a free annual copy of your report from each of the three bureaus listed below. To request it, visit www.annualcreditreport.com. If you want to know your credit score—the number used to measure your creditworthiness in comparison with other borrowers—you'll have to purchase it for a small fee. You can do this when you request your free annual credit report, or by contacting one of the major credit bureaus listed here:

- Experian: www.experian.com
- TransUnion: www.transunion.com
- Equifax: www.equifax.com.

CD EXTRA!

Write an elevator speech. You should be able to do a great job of selling your business idea to anyone in the time it takes to travel between floors on an elevator. Look on the CD-ROM for the bonus article "Write Your Elevator Speech," which will help you craft a perfect pitch.

Be honest, patient, flexible, and persistent. It can be hard to get a lender's attention and you may encounter delays. Do your best to understand that the lender may have more loan requests than time available. But do persist. This can be a good time to be a polite but squeaky wheel. Your lender will have a hard time ignoring you if you call each week with new, exciting information about your business. If you make your best effort and still can't get an answer to your request, turn your attention to other lenders.

Small Business Banking Services

If you're talking to a banker about financing options, you might want to check out what other services are available for your business, including:

- checking accounts
- savings and money market accounts
- online banking
- debit cards (also called business check cards)
- credit cards
- merchant card services (this enables you to accept customer credit cards)
- night deposits
- tax payment processing, and
- fraud protection.

Writing a Business Plan

Always plan ahead. It wasn't raining when Noah built the ark.

—RICHARD C. CUSHING

A business plan is the blueprint for your business—a document you create to ensure that your enterprise will be strong and structurally sound. It sets out details about how your business will operate and provides financial data to show how it will turn a profit.

You may write a business plan for your own use—to help you start and manage the business—or you may write it to convince others to lend you money. Either way, it's an essential task to complete before you open your doors.

Writing a plan for yourself. Because most retirement businesses require only modest funding from others—if any—you'll probably be writing a simple business plan for your own use. If so, your plan will consist of a basic outline of your business, including its goals and how you intend to meet them. You'll describe your products and services, customer base, competition, and marketing strategies. But the heart of your plan will be your financial projections, including:

- an estimate of start-up costs
- a profit-and-loss forecast (a month-by-month picture of the revenues and expenses during your business's first year), and
- a cash-flow projection (even if your profit numbers look good, you'll need this forecast to be sure you'll have cash on hand to cover your expenses each month).

If most of these topics look familiar, that's good! As you worked through the earlier chapters in this book, you completed much of what you'll need to include in your business plan. Crafting a formal plan will help you get organized and build on what you've already done.

If you don't expect to use your business plan to seek financing from others, you may be tempted to cut corners when you put it together—or skip it altogether. That's not a good idea. First, your business plan is key to keeping your venture organized and on track. Second, even if you don't plan to borrow money, you may want to show some or all of your plan to others. Your business plan can be a great way to introduce yourself to suppliers, contractors, potential employees, and even key customers. So it's well worth the time to make it clear, clean, and complete.

Writing a plan for lenders. If you will use your plan to borrow money for your business, you'll need to step it up a bit. Besides the details listed above, your plan will need to include a well-crafted introduction and a request for funds. You'll want to take extra care when it comes to describing your customers, evaluating your competitors, delivering a knock-out marketing strategy, and proving that you'll make a profit. It's also not a bad idea to include a resume of your business accomplishments. Essentially, you want to show potential lenders that your business will be a smashing success and that you're the right person to make it happen.

RESOURCE

Getting help with your business plan. When you're ready to write your business plan, check out *How to Write a Business Plan*, by Mike McKeever (Nolo). It shows you, step by step, how to craft your plan and present it to potential investors. The book includes sample plans and a CD-ROM with spreadsheets to help you determine and forecast sales revenue, profit and loss, and cash flow. Or, you might want to use computer software to help you write your plan. *Business Plan Pro* (Palo Alto Software) is one of the leading packages, including hundreds of sample plans and easy-to-use worksheets. You can find both of these products on Nolo's website at www.nolo.com.

Finally, if you will submit or show your plan to potential lenders, colleagues, or customers, you may want to consider asking a professional (like a business counselor at your local Small Business Development Center) to review it for you. If numbers aren't your strong point, a good accountant can make sure your figures are accurate and clearly presented. And a professional writer with small business experience can help you polish your plan until it shines.

Summing Up

Deciding how to finance your business will help you get off to a good start. There are two parts to your decision: how much money you need and where you'll get it. The following Tool lets you summarize your financing plan and list the tasks you need to complete.

First, refer to Reality Check #4 in Chapter 10. There, you estimated the total cash needed to start your business. Update your figures as needed and write that amount in the Tool below.

Second, use the Tool to summarize where you'll get the cash you need. Refer to your profile for the amount of money you are willing to invest, updating the figure if needed. Then list which of your personal resources you plan to tap for money—and any related tasks you need to complete. For example, if you plan to withdraw money from your 401(k), you might need to contact your plan administrator or complete paperwork. If you plan to borrow against a whole life insurance policy, you might list "call insurance broker."

If you won't use outside sources of financing, you can skip the remainder of the Tool. Otherwise, list the amount of money you'll need from others, identify possible sources, and write down related tasks—including writing a business plan.

FINANCING YOUR BUSINESS

Total cash needed to start my business: $__________________

	Possible Sources of Funds	Tasks
Amount I can invest: $______________	1. ______________ 2. ______________ 3. ______________	1. ______________ 2. ______________ 3. ______________
Amount I must get from others: $ ______________	1. ______________ 2. ______________ 3. ______________	1. ______________ 2. ______________ 3. ______________

CHAPTER

13

Learn About Taxes

The hardest thing to understand in the world is the income tax.
—ALBERT EINSTEIN

Yes, you'll have to pay taxes. Yes, the tax laws are complicated. And of course you don't want to pay more than you have to.

However, successful small business owners know that their main focus should be running their business, not minimizing taxes. Good business decisions are seldom made when saving taxes is the key factor.

Still, you have the right to take advantage of every tax-saving law that you can. You may need professional help with that, but you can keep both your tax and accounting costs down if you have at least some understanding of income tax basics. In this chapter, we introduce tax laws that might apply to you and your business and give you resources for further investigation. At the end of the chapter, you'll find a Tool to help you keep track of your tax-related tasks.

Types of Taxes

When you turned to this chapter, you were probably thinking of income taxes. Indeed, they will be your primary tax concern and probably the most expensive and complicated of all the taxes you and your business will pay. However, there are many other taxes that may apply to your venture, including:

- **Real property taxes.** Your business will pay taxes on any real property (real estate) it owns, as you do on your home. These taxes are levied by state and local governments.
- **Personal property taxes.** Some state and local governments tax the value of personal property owned by businesses. Personal property includes the things your business owns that are not categorized as real property, such as furniture, machinery, equipment, or tools.
- **Employer payroll taxes.** If your business has employees, you must pay federal, state, and local employer payroll taxes. This is true even if you form a corporation and become its only employee. Most

employer payroll taxes are a percentage of the gross wages earned by each employee. These taxes include Social Security, Medicare, and unemployment taxes. (Some business owners must cover their own Social Security and Medicare taxes. It's called the Self-Employment tax—more about that below). Your business may also be required to pay for workers' compensation insurance. This varies by state and can be quite expensive.

- **Employee payroll taxes.** Employees are also responsible for payroll taxes. These won't cost you or your business anything, but you must withhold these taxes from employee paychecks and deposit the money with the appropriate government agency. Employee payroll taxes generally include federal and state income taxes, Social Security, and Medicare.
- **Sales tax.** You may be required to collect sales tax on the products or services you sell. Be sure to check for local as well as state sales taxes.
- **Other taxes.** There may be other federal, state, or local taxes that apply to your business. For example, your state or local government may tax tobacco products, alcoholic beverages, gasoline, and lodging.

You'll have to do some research to find out which of these taxes will apply to your business. We've included some resources at the end of the chapter. You can also check with your state department of revenue and county treasurer, or similar agencies in your locale.

The Income Tax System

The difference between death and taxes is death doesn't get worse every time Congress meets.

—WILL ROGERS

In a nutshell, income taxes are based on your taxable income, which is calculated by deducting expenses from revenues. You multiply your taxable income by your tax rate to determine your total tax bill. You'll probably be responsible for both federal and state income taxes, so you'll want to familiarize yourself with the rules that apply to both.

Some tax provisions depend on the form of ownership you choose for your business. As mentioned in the previous chapter, if you set up your business as a sole proprietorship, partnership, or S corporation, you will pay income tax personally at your individual tax rate. If you form a corporation, the business itself pays taxes using corporate tax rates, which tend to be lower than individual rates. You'll pay tax on any dividends or salary you receive from the corporation. For limited liability companies, you have a choice to be taxed like a corporation or a sole proprietorship.

Important Deductions for Small Businesses

You might be entitled to some or all of the following tax deductions, among others:

- **Home office deduction.** If you use part of your home exclusively and regularly for business, you may be able to deduct some household costs, such as a portion of your rent, utilities, and insurance.
- **Travel, meals, and entertainment.** In general, you can deduct expenses you incur while on business away from home—for example, transportation, lodging, and tips. However, you can deduct only 50% of your costs for business-related meals and entertainment. This applies whether you are traveling or just taking a client to lunch in your hometown.
- **Auto expenses.** You can deduct expenses for business-related driving —using your actual costs or a standard mileage rate established by the IRS. Keep a mileage log in your glove box and be sure to fill it in for each business trip, including the date, number of miles, destination, and purpose.
- **Medical insurance.** You may be able to deduct the cost of medical and dental insurance premiums covering you, your spouse, and dependents.

Whatever form of business you choose, the good news about income tax is that many, many business expenses are deductible. You can deduct any expense that the IRS considers "ordinary, necessary, and reasonable," including costs for equipment, supplies, advertising, rent, utilities, telephone, professional fees, travel, and much more. The bad news is that the law—not your personal wishes—determines which revenues are taxable and which expenses are deductible.

Especially if this is your first business, you probably won't know what's taxable, what's deductible, and what's not. Keep track of everything, just in case, and start educating yourself right away. The self-help resources listed at the end of this chapter provide many of the details—and suggestions for organizing them. If you have questions, seek clarification from an accountant or a lawyer who's familiar with tax laws.

Make Sure It's a Business, Not a Hobby

You can't deduct expenses or losses if your business isn't really a business. If your venture is profitable in at least three of five consecutive tax years, the IRS presumes it's a business. But if you don't meet this test, the government might take a closer look. Do you keep thorough business records and have a separate business bank account? How much effort do you put into marketing and advertising? Do you have all the necessary licenses and permits? If you're not sure whether your business will pass muster with the IRS, add this to the list of issues to discuss with an accountant or qualified legal expert.

CAUTION

Listen to Uncle Sam, not Cousin Joe. Your personal tax situation will take into account the income from your business, other forms of retirement income, your spouse's earnings, and more. The calculation is highly individualized. Friends and family may have lots of advice, but tax-saving methods that work well for one taxpayer don't always help another. If Cousin Joe is a CPA, you might do well to accept his suggestions—just make sure your guidance is coming from an objective expert.

Self-Employment Tax

Employers withhold Social Security and Medicare taxes from employee paychecks, then match those amounts dollar-for-dollar and send it all to the federal government. As a self-employed business owner, you must pay into Social Security and Medicare as both the employer and the employee. This is called the self-employment tax.

Self-employment tax applies to sole proprietors and most partners, but may not apply if your business is a corporation or limited liability company. In fact, some business owners organize as a limited liability company in part to avoid the self-employment tax. You may want to consider this question when selecting the best form for your business.

If you are liable for self-employment tax, you must pay it if your business earns $400 or more in a calendar year. The Medicare portion of the tax is 2.9% of all profits you make in your business. For 2007, Social Security is 12.4% of the first $97,500 of your profits (this dollar amount increases each year).

There is some tax relief if you must pay self-employment tax: You can deduct one-half of the tax when calculating your taxable income.

For more information about self-employment tax, talk to your accountant or consult the resources listed at the end of this chapter.

Estimated Tax Payments

Years ago, Congress created our pay-as-you-go tax system. For employees, this means that income taxes are withheld from every paycheck. If you're a business owner, you might not draw a paycheck, but the government still wants its money sooner rather than later. You'll pay-as-you-go by making an estimated tax payment every quarter.

Sole proprietorship, partnership, S corporation, or LLC with personal taxation. You must make estimated tax payments if you expect to owe at least $1,000 in federal income tax for the year, including self-employment taxes. Your payments are due on April 15, June 15, September 15, and January 15.

Corporation or LLC taxed like a corporation. You may draw a paycheck from your business and pay your personal income taxes that way, but the business itself will have to make quarterly estimated payments if it expects net income of $500 or more. Payments are due on April 15, June 15, September 15, and December 15.

Avoiding Penalties

No matter what type of business you have, you'll face penalties if you don't make your estimated tax payment on time—or if you don't pay enough. Your total estimated tax payments must equal the lower of:

- 100% of the total tax you owed the previous year, or
- 90% of the tax you'll owe for the current year.

This last calculation can be tricky. If you want to use it, you may want to turn to a self-help resource or an accountant for help. You'll also want to be sure that you've got enough cash on hand to cover your estimated payments. Perhaps you'll need a separate bank account, monthly set-asides, or automatic payments. Your accountant can help you determine the strategy that's right for you.

Taxes on Social Security Benefits

Social Security benefits are normally tax-free. But if your income goes over a threshold, your benefits will be taxed. Unfortunately, income from a successful retirement business might push you over that threshold—so some of your Social Security benefits could go right back to the government.

To find out whether your Social Security benefits will be taxed, you have to determine your combined income. This is your income from all sources other than Social Security, plus one-half of your Social Security benefits. If your combined income for the calendar year exceeds the threshold published by the IRS, your benefits will be taxed on your personal income tax return. (For 2007, the figures are $25,000 if you're single and $32,000 if you are married and filing jointly.) You'll pay even higher taxes if your combined income exceeds $34,000 (single) or $32,000 (married filing jointly)—in that case, up to 85% of your benefits could be taxed.

There are ways to keep your business income out of this calculation; for example, by incorporating and limiting the amount you take out of the business. This can be tricky, so check with a tax professional if this issue concerns you.

Federal Tax Identification Number

The government requires many businesses to obtain an Employer Identification Number (EIN). Corporations, limited liability companies, and partnerships generally must have an EIN. Sole proprietors without employees do not need this number—instead, they use the owner's Social Security number as the business identification number. If you do get an EIN, you'll put it on all business-related tax returns and deposits. To apply for an EIN, go to the IRS website at www.irs.gov and complete Form SS-4.

Other Reasons to Get an EIN

You might want to get an EIN for your business even if you're not required to. Here's why:

- **Selling products or services to organizations.** Many organizations keep their supplier information by EIN—trying to use your Social Security number instead can be a hassle.
- **Keeping your Social Security number private.** One way to avoid identity theft is to limit use of your Social Security number. An EIN can help you protect your sensitive personal information.

RESOURCE

More information about taxes. To learn more about small business taxes, you can start with the articles on Nolo's website at www.nolo.com. You'll find free, detailed information on tax topics from understanding deductions to surviving a tax audit. To handle questions as they arise, you might consider keeping one or more of these Nolo books by your side as you start your new business:

Tax Savvy for Small Business, by Frederick Daily, provides an in-depth look at federal business taxes and shows small business owners how to make the right tax decisions.

Working for Yourself: Law & Taxes for Independent Contractors, Freelancers & Consultants, by Stephen Fishman, is specifically designed for self-employed individuals who offer their services on a contract basis.

Deduct It! Lower Your Small Business Taxes, by Stephen Fishman, provides key information and strategies for keeping your tax bill under control.

Home Business Tax Deductions: Keep What You Earn, by Stephen Fishman, is a comprehensive guide to taxes for small business owners who operate from home.

Finally, don't hesitate to go straight to the source for tax rules and information. Visit the IRS website at www.irs.gov and click on the "Business" link. The IRS offers helpful articles for small business owners and a host of free publications. Publication 4591, *Small Business Federal Tax Responsibilities*, is a reference list of IRS Web resources and publications helpful for small business owners, including:

- Publication 334, *Tax Guide for Small Business*
- Publication 535, *Business Expenses*
- Publication 583, *Starting a Business and Keeping Records*
- Publication 587, *Business Use of Your Home*, and
- Circular E, *Employer's Tax Guide.*

TAX CHECKLIST

❑ I know and understand the types of taxes that will apply to my business. These include:

Federal and State Income Taxes	yes ❑	no ❑
Real Property Taxes	yes ❑	no ❑
Personal Property Taxes	yes ❑	no ❑
Employer Payroll Taxes	yes ❑	no ❑
Sales Taxes	yes ❑	no ❑
Other Taxes: ____________________	yes ❑	no ❑

❑ I understand how my business will be taxed (separately or on my personal income tax return).

❑ I understand how much self-employment tax I'm likely to pay.

❑ I have estimated additional income tax I'll pay if my Social Security benefits are taxed.

❑ I know how much in quarterly estimated income tax I'll need to pay, and I've set up a system to make sure I'll have the money on hand to do so.

❑ I have evaluated whether my venture will be classified as a hobby rather than a business and understand the consequences.

❑ I have learned about deductions that may apply to my business and understand potential limitations on those deductions.

❑ I have explored legitimate means to minimize my taxes.

❑ I have obtained my federal Employer Identification Number, if required.

❑ I have set up my record keeping systems, including a mileage log for my car, if necessary.

CHAPTER

Find the Best Health Insurance

The first wealth is health.

—RALPH WALDO EMERSON

Medical bills can turn a comfortable retirement living into a budget nightmare. No wonder so many people list health insurance coverage as one of their main retirement concerns.

The best health insurance coverage for you depends on your financial situation, health conditions, and former employment. It's not one size fits all, so it pays to explore your options. Here are three steps you can take:

1. **Consider Medicare.** Medicare is the primary insurance coverage for many retirees; it applies once you've turned age 65. There are choices within this system, including buying supplemental insurance and prescription drug coverage.
2. **Look into group plans.** The core principle behind a group plan is that the high- and low-cost participants balance out. The risk is spread, so you are protected against exclusion or having your premiums increased just because your health worsens. You might be able to get group insurance through your former employer, your spouse's employer, or a professional association.
3. **Check out individual insurance policies.** If you're not eligible for Medicare and don't have access to a group plan, an individual plan might be your only insurance option. These plans are generally more expensive than group plans—and sometimes they don't cover as much. However, there are high-deductible policies and health savings plans that can make an individual policy a workable option.

Unfortunately, health insurance can be complicated—but the right plan can save you a bundle of money and get you the coverage you want, so it's well worth learning more. This chapter gets you started and gives you a Tool to help organize your search and find the best health insurance for you.

Medicare

Medicare is health insurance sponsored by the federal government for people age 65 or older and for younger people with certain disabilities. It's divided into four parts, lettered A through D. You're covered by some of these parts automatically; for others, you choose whether or not to participate. And some of these parts let you choose your coverage and costs.

Medicare Part A. Medicare Part A covers hospital, home health, hospice, and nursing facility care and lets you choose your doctors. If you or your spouse paid at least ten years of Medicare taxes while working, you will not pay a monthly premium for Medicare Part A. If you did not pay these taxes, you can still purchase Part A insurance.

If you are receiving Social Security, you will be automatically enrolled in Medicare Part A on the first day of the month you turn 65. If you aren't yet receiving Social Security and are nearing age 65, you should sign up for Medicare Part A during the three months before your birthday month. Your enrollment period extends another three months, but it's best to start the process as early as possible.

Medicare Part B. If you are 65 and receiving Social Security benefits, you'll also be enrolled in Medicare Part B. This insurance covers routine care such as doctor visits, lab tests, outpatient hospital care, and medical equipment. Like Part A, you have choice of physicians. You'll have to pay for this insurance and the rates change every year. You can opt out of this program—and you may wish to do so if you have insurance coverage from another source. However, signing up for Plan B coverage later might result in higher premiums.

Medicare Part C. This is a combination of Part A and Part B (and often Part D) coverage in one package called a Medicare Advantage Plan. These plans are sold by private insurance companies and usually operate as an HMO or PPO (for more about these terms, see "Individual Health Care Plans," below). Medicare Advantage Plans offer lower out-of-pocket costs and more coverage, but restrict your choice of doctors. The plans differ in coverage and cost, so you'll need to evaluate them closely to see which one is best for your circumstances.

Medicare Part D. Historically, Medicare did not pay for prescription drugs. In light of the dramatic increases in drug costs, a new program for prescription drugs began in 2006, covered under Medicare Part D. This program is complicated and has caused much confusion, so look for changes as Congress and regulators try to sort out the details.

Medicare Part D allows participants to choose from a variety of plans. Monthly premiums and copayments vary, although it is estimated that up to one-third of seniors will qualify for assistance and receive the benefits with little or no cost. If you are interested in a Medicare prescription drug plan, carefully check to be sure it covers the medications you're likely to need. Pay attention to the fine print—some plans even dictate the pharmacies you must use.

Medigap insurance. Medicare does not cover all health care costs. That's why many retirees carry supplemental insurance, called Medigap. This insurance is sold by private insurance companies, so you'll need to consult an insurance professional to learn more.

Medicaid. Low-income retirees and those with limited resources may qualify for Medicaid. This program covers many of the costs not covered by Medicare and varies from state to state.

RESOURCE

Help with Medicare and Medicaid. The best resources for learning more about these government insurance plans are The Centers for Medicare and Medicaid Services at www.cms.hhs.gov and the Medicare website at www.medicare.gov. You can read or order publications and compare plans online.

Group Plans

If you're not yet eligible for Medicare, your best option for health insurance is probably a group plan. The specifics—coverage, cost, choice of providers—vary greatly from plan to plan. However, in almost all cases, group plans give you the best coverage at the lowest cost.

Employer-Sponsored Plans

The majority of group health insurance plans are sponsored by employers. Of course, if you're reading this book, there's a good chance that you're no longer working for someone else or that you're going to be on your own soon—but some employer-sponsored plans cover retirees. If you have one of these plans, consider yourself very fortunate. The number of such plans is declining rapidly. In 1988, almost 66% of companies offered retiree health coverage. By 2003, the number had fallen to 38%—and it continues to drop each year.

If your spouse or partner is still working and has medical insurance coverage, find out whether you can be covered, too. Adding a new family member can sometimes mean a waiting period or more limited coverage, so—if possible—look into the specifics well in advance of your retirement. You might wish to be covered by your spouse even while you're still working so that you'll have insurance right away when you retire.

Even if you are still covered by an employer-sponsored plan, you're likely to experience rising required contributions, higher copayments, and reduced benefits. One study predicted that by 2031 employers will pay only 10% of retiree health care costs.

Sticking with your employer's plan is especially beneficial if you have preexisting conditions or are taking expensive prescription drugs. If you're in this situation, see below for information about COBRA—a law that can help you keep your employer-sponsored health insurance after you retire.

COBRA

COBRA (Consolidated Omnibus Reconciliation Act of 1985) is a federal law that allows you to keep your insurance coverage for up to 18 months if you lose your job, quit, or retire. To qualify, you must have worked for an employer with 20 or more employees, or for your state or local government. Your family members are also eligible for continued coverage if they were covered while you were employed. Keep in mind that the law does not require your former employer to pay for your coverage.

To learn more about COBRA, go to the U.S. Department of Labor website at www.dol.gov/dol/topic/health-plans/cobra.htm. COBRA is complex and you may want more advice about how the law applies to you. Talk to the human resource manager or benefits officer at the company you are leaving or consult an insurance adviser.

Association Group Plans

Owning a business can open the door to joining trade or professional associations, such as the National Restaurant Association, the American Institute of Certified Public Accountants, or the Consumer Electronics Association. Many of these groups offer insurance plans—but you should thoroughly investigate before you sign up. Longstanding organizations that do more than just offer health insurance—for example, associations that provide education, sponsor industry promotions, or lobby lawmakers—are probably your best bet. If an organization is established only to sponsor health insurance, use caution. Many do not actually offer the protections of a group plan, but instead operate more like individual plans. That means you won't get the low- and high-cost participant balance typical of group plans—and you could face increased premiums or cancellation of your insurance if you incur large medical expenses.

In addition, associations may fall outside the jurisdiction of your state insurance laws. Although being regulated or licensed won't guarantee that an insurer is offering you a good plan, it does lend legitimacy. Many states have cracked down on unscrupulous plan operators, so ask your state insurance commissioner about any complaints, investigations, or disciplinary actions before choosing an association's plan.

RESOURCE

How to contact your state insurance commissioner. You can find a link to your state's website by visiting the National Association of Insurance Commissioners at www.naic.org.

Individual Health Care Plans

You might not be eligible for Medicare or a group plan, in which case you'll have to turn to an individual plan for your insurance coverage. There are many companies offering these plans, from well-known national companies to smaller, regional companies. It's very important to shop around—coverage and costs vary widely.

There are several different types of individual health care coverage:

- **Fee-for-service insurance.** This insurance pays a portion of your health care costs and you pay the remainder. You might cover your part by making a copayment at the time of service or the insurance company might bill you for your share. You can usually choose your physician, but that privilege may increase your monthly premiums.
- **Health maintenance organization (HMO) or preferred provider organization (PPO).** With an HMO or PPO, the plan pays your medical costs and you incur only a small copayment when you receive care. However, your choice of physicians is limited. In an HMO, you're usually limited to using just the physicians and hospitals belonging to the plan's network. PPOs often allow you to seek services outside the network, but you'll pay a bigger share of the total cost. Because your choice of providers is reduced, HMOs and PPOs are usually cheaper than fee-for-service plans.

- **High-risk pool.** This type of insurance is available in more than 30 states. You can get insurance through a high-risk pool if you have been turned down by insurance companies, or were unable to buy insurance with a lower monthly premium than what the high-risk pool would charge you. The rules vary by state, so check with your state insurance commissioner (see the contact information, above) to see if a high-risk pool might work for you.

Evaluating Health Insurance Plans

There are many questions you should ask before buying health insurance. Here are some of the most important:

- How much are the monthly premiums?
- Which services are covered or excluded? What percentage of various medical services will the policy pay? (Consider hospitalization, emergency room service, routine surgery, doctor visits, dental charges, vision, mental health, home health care, preventive care, routine physicals, medical equipment, and supplies.)
- Is there a deductible or copayment?
- What is the prescription drug benefit?
- Are there annual or lifetime limits to how much the plan will pay?
- Will preexisting conditions be covered? Will premiums go up because of them?
- Are there waiting periods?
- Can you choose your health care providers? Can you keep your present doctor? Will you and your doctor have control over medical decisions?
- Will the plan cover you if you travel out of town?
- Will the plan cover your spouse, partner, or dependents?
- What is the reputation of this insurance carrier? Does the company have a history of quick and reliable payment? Is the company licensed in and regulated by the state?
- Is the policy renewable at your option?

HIPAA

Many people know HIPAA (the Health Insurance Portability and Accountability Act) as the federal law that guards the privacy of sensitive medical information. But HIPAA can also help you if you are switching insurance plans—either from one group plan to another or from a group plan to an individual plan. Here's what it can do:

- protect you against denial due to preexisting conditions
- prohibit higher monthly charges just because of those conditions, and
- limit how long you must wait for coverage (generally no more than 12 months).

These protections can help you get the insurance coverage you need. Understand, however, that the law does not limit what the insurance company can charge you, force former employers to pay premiums for you, or dictate what kind of coverage you can get.

To take advantage of HIPAA's protections, the following must be true:

- You have had health insurance through a group plan, a health maintenance organization (HMO), an individual insurance policy, Medicaid, or Medicare.
- Your former group plan was covered by HIPAA (most are).
- You have not gone without health insurance coverage for more than 63 days since your previous plan ended.
- If you are moving to an individual plan, you have participated for at least 18 months in your previous plan. You also must not be able to get Medicare, Medicaid, or be able to join a group plan. You cannot have other health insurance and you must have used up any extension of group insurance you got under COBRA or state law.

Health Savings Accounts

Many retirees buy health insurance with a very high deductible. They pay for routine medical costs–such as doctor visits, lab fees, and prescription medications—themselves. If that is your insurance strategy, you might consider a Health Savings Account (HSA).

With an HSA, you purchase lower-premium, high-deductible health insurance and then stash away dollars into an investment account that you control. You can use the money to pay for medical costs that your insurance does not cover.

HSAs are newcomers on the market, but they are gaining popularity. More than 4.5 million Americans were enrolled in HSAs in 2007, mostly through employers, but the plans are gaining favor with self-employed folks, too. Many who have HSAs feel that they can more actively control their medical costs. They ask more questions, comparison shop, and are more inclined to take care of their health, since both their savings and their health are at risk.

The amount you can contribute to your HSA is limited (to $2,900 for individuals and $5,800 for families in 2008, plus an additional $900 if you are 55 or older). You get an income tax deduction for the amount you contribute, even if you do not itemize deductions on your tax return. The earnings in your HSA are tax-free.

You can take money out of the account to pay for medical costs, which is defined broadly enough to include some nonprescription drugs and alternative medicine therapies. Unlike many flexible-spending accounts offered by employers, you don't have to use up the account balance each year. If there are unused funds in your account at the end of the year, the amounts simply roll into the next year. However, If you use the money to pay for nonmedical expenses before you reach the age of 65, you'll have to pay tax on the withdrawal plus a 10% penalty. After age 65, you pay tax on the money you withdraw but the penalty is waived.

Talk with your current insurer to find out whether your insurance policy is HSA compatible. If you have a financial or tax adviser, discuss the pros and cons of these plans.

RESOURCE

More information about Health Savings Accounts. The following websites can help you find and compare banks, brokers, and insurance companies offering Health Savings Accounts:

- www.hsainsider.com
- www.hsadecisions.org
- www.nahu.org
- www.eHealthInsurance.com.

RESOURCE

Understanding your medical insurance options. If you're still confused about medical insurance, you're not alone. Here are some places to get help:

AARP. Explore AARP's online resources at www.aarp.org/health. You'll find materials to help you understand Medicare and valuable hints on what to do if you're losing your group plan insurance.

State Health Insurance Assistance Programs. You can get individualized help with Medicare from your State Health Insurance Assistance Program. Get the phone number or link from the Medicare website at www.medicare.gov.

U.S. Department of Labor. Visit www.dol.gov to check out helpful brochures such as *Life Changes Require Health Choices: Know your Benefit Options.*

Insurance brokers. If your current insurance agent doesn't handle health insurance, get a referral. If you can't make a connection that way, you might try the Association of Health Insurance Advisors at www.ahia.net.

RESOURCE

Books about medical insurance. Here are two books you can consult for a comprehensive review of health insurance options:

The New Health Insurance Solution: How to get Cheaper, Better Coverage Without a Traditional Employer Plan, by Paul Zane Pilzer (Wiley), discusses health insurance options and ways to save money if you don't have a traditional employer-sponsored insurance plan.

Healthcare for Less: Getting the Care You Need Without Breaking the Bank, by Michelle Katz (Hatherleigh), reviews simple, cost-effective ways to get the coverage you need.

HEALTH INSURANCE CHECKLIST

- ❑ I have read and understand official publications about Medicare, Medicaid, and Medigap insurance.
- ❑ I have reviewed my COBRA and HIPAA options with the benefits officer at my current workplace.
- ❑ I understand the retiree health insurance benefit offered by my employer.
- ❑ I understand how coverage might be obtained through my spouse's employer.
- ❑ I have examined group plans offered through trade or professional associations I plan to join.
- ❑ I have evaluated my options for an individual health insurance plan.
- ❑ I have evaluated Health Savings Accounts and understand whether such an account is right for me.
- ❑ I have a realistic idea of how much I will need to spend monthly for health insurance and medical costs.

Where to Get More Help

It's hard work to start and run a business and there will be times when you need a little help. This chapter points you toward resources that small business owners often use to tackle their business challenges. We set out some common situations in which you may want to seek professional assistance and we give you suggestions for finding the best advisers—from attorneys, accountants, and small business services to self-help books, software, and websites.

Professional Advisers

First-time business owners often feel uncertain about whether and when to use an attorney or accountant. A few use professionals to handle all of their legal and accounting needs and others take care of everything themselves. Most fall somewhere in between these two extremes. This section highlights the situations in which these experts can help you. If you don't already have a good attorney or accountant on your team, we provide some tips for finding one.

Attorneys

An experienced small business attorney can give you legal advice and prepare legal documents for you. If you feel confident tackling basic legal matters on your own, you may be able to turn to self-help guides for assistance (see the end of this chapter) and call your lawyer only if you hit a snag. However, some small business owners feel more comfortable (or just less burdened) if they involve a lawyer in their business from the start, turning over tasks such as:

- forming a corporation, LLC, or partnership
- registering a business name
- registering copyrights, trademarks, or patents
- preparing legal documents, such as contracts and noncompete agreements, that others will sign
- reviewing legal documents, such as contracts and real estate leases, that others have asked you to sign, and
- reviewing equipment leases and loan documents.

When it comes to working with a lawyer on tasks like the ones listed above, you may be able to share the load. For example, it may be possible for you to prepare your own documents and have your lawyer review them. It is becoming increasingly common for lawyers to offer these kinds of "coaching" arrangements. If you're interested, ask your lawyer whether he or she will work with you in this way.

Legal Document Preparation Centers

These centers are a low-cost alternative to attorneys for some legal matters. They cannot offer legal advice or review legal documents but can help you prepare documents, such as incorporation or LLC formation paperwork. You complete a questionnaire or worksheet and an assistant prepares your document based on your information. Look for legal document preparation centers or paralegals in the yellow pages of your phone book or on the Internet.

Accountants

There are many types of accountants to help you and your business. Let's start by looking at what an accountant can do for you. Among other things, an accountant can help you:

- prepare a financial plan for your retirement
- select and set up a system for record keeping and business accounting
- keep your daily, weekly, or monthly books
- create a personal and business tax plan
- prepare annual tax returns
- respond to an IRS or state tax agency audit
- calculate and prepare quarterly estimated tax payments
- prepare financial statements
- calculate financial projections for loan applications, and
- process payroll, if your business has employees.

The type of accountant to use depends on how much help you need and how much you are willing to pay. Here are the types of professionals you're likely to encounter when searching for help with your personal and business finances:

- **CPA (Certified Public Accountant)**. CPAs provide the widest range of services—at the greatest cost. They must complete rigorous education and licensing requirements and pass a national examination. In most states, only a CPA can perform an independent audit or review of a business. It's unlikely that you'll need a CPA's most specialized services, although sometimes a review is required by loan agreements or other contracts. A CPA can also provide expert assistance with tax planning and preparation. Many specialize in taxation issues for small business owners. And a CPA can help you with your business plan and loan applications.
- **PA (Public Accountant).** In some states, a person can be licensed as a public accountant. These accountants usually have less rigorous education and licensing requirements and charge less than CPAs. They can do a wide variety of accounting work, from bookkeeping to payroll to income tax preparation, but may specialize in one particular task or industry. You might wish to consult a PA for help setting up your accounting systems.
- **EA (Enrolled Agent).** The Enrolled Agent is a national license for those specializing in income taxes. These accountants have passed a two-day examination or have worked full-time for the IRS at least five years. They're a good bet for help with your income taxes, but they don't usually do bookkeeping or set up accounting systems.
- **LTC (Licensed Tax Consultant) and LTP (Licensed Tax Preparer).** These accountants primarily prepare tax returns. Licensing requirements and what type of work they can do is determined by state law and varies widely.
- **Bookkeeper.** Bookkeepers generally record day-to-day transactions and produce monthly reports, often taking care of accounts payable, accounts receivable, and payroll. State law determines whether they can prepare tax returns. There usually is no licensing or education

requirement for bookkeepers. They typically charge less per hour than the other types of accountants listed above.

Finding an Attorney or Accountant

How will you find the best attorney or accountant? Thumbing through the phone book or doing an Internet search is unlikely to be efficient or satisfying. Instead, look to the following individuals or organizations for referrals:

- **Your personal attorney or accountant.** If you've used a lawyer or accountant for personal matters, ask whether he or she has small business expertise. If not, ask for a referral to an expert.
- **Family and friends.** Ask people you know if they've got a great attorney or accountant. If you get a name or two, follow up to see whether they have the experience you need or can send you to someone else who does.
- **Other small business owners.** Talk to successful business owners who face issues like yours. Chances are you'll find someone who has had experience with local legal and financial experts.
- **Your Chamber of Commerce or Small Business Development Center.** These organizations usually prefer to list several possibilities rather than recommend a single name, but that's okay. It's a good idea to talk with several possible candidates before you settle on one.
- **Trade associations.** Talk to representatives of your trade association, especially if industry-specific expertise is important.
- **Your banker.** If you have an established relationship with a banker that you trust, ask for recommendations.
- **Professional directories.** You can find a large number of directories on the Internet. Use these with caution, being sure to interview and carefully assess each candidate. If you're looking for a lawyer, you might want to visit Nolo's lawyer directory at www.nolo.com. Each lawyer posts a detailed profile to help you get started with your evaluation. The directory is currently available in only a handful of states, but new locations are being added regularly.

Think of your relationship with a lawyer or accountant as a long-term commitment. Trust is very important. You must feel comfortable discussing important and sometimes private issues with your advisers.

Interview at least three candidates before choosing an expert. Make sure the interview is part of a free initial consultation. You don't want to be billed before any real work is done.

You can use the following list of questions when interviewing attorneys and accountants. If a candidate is unwilling or unable to satisfactorily answer your questions, keep looking.

What to Ask an Attorney or Accountant

- What is the focus of your practice? In what areas do you specialize?
- How long have you been serving small business clients?
- What experience do you have with businesses in my industry? Do you have any current clients in my industry?
- What do you see as the major issues I face in starting and operating my business?
- What services do you typically perform for clients monthly? Quarterly? Annually?
- How often do you generally meet with a client like me?
- Will you meet with me or will I see someone on your staff?
- What do you find interesting about me and my business?
- What are your fees and how do you calculate them?

Keeping Fees Low

Even if you find a great lawyer or accountant, you'll want to do all that you can to keep fees under control. Here are some tips:

- **Be prepared.** Bring an agenda or list of your questions. Be sure you understand the issues.

- **Review several issues each time you meet.**
- **Get advice before you have a problem.** Read industry trade publications and other resources to keep up to date with legal and tax changes that may need your attention.
- **Keep complete and accurate records.**
- **Buy self-help materials** that include standard legal agreements. Draft legal documents yourself and have your attorney review them.
- **Use more than one type of accountant,** matching cost to the level of service you need. For example, a bookkeeper is probably cheaper for payroll services than your CPA, but you may want your CPA's help with tax planning.
- **Use other professionals** (bankers, insurance agents, real estate brokers) who do not charge for their advice.
- **Establish that you are a valuable client.** Pay your bills on time. If you're happy with your adviser's services, create goodwill by referring other clients.

Small Business Development Centers and Other Services

Federal, state, and local government agencies provide numerous services for small business owners. For general assistance, your best bet is a local Small Business Development Center.

Small Business Development Centers serve more than 1.3 million small business owners each year, offering low-cost seminars on a wide variety of business topics. They also provide free one-on-one counseling. Most SBDCs are hosted at a university or community college. Find the nearest center by visiting the national SBDC website at www.asbdc-us.org.

You also can seek help from these organizations:

- **SBA.** The U.S. Small Business Administration offers many free publications and online training. Find its website at www.sba.org.

- **SCORE.** The Service Corps of Retired Executives is a voluntary, nonprofit organization with chapters throughout the country. Members have extensive business experience and will counsel you free of charge either in person or online. Visit score at www.score.org.
- **University sponsored programs.** You might be able to get help from a smart student studying business or entrepreneurship. Students often complete projects for local businesses as part of their curriculum. Contact nearby colleges to see if they sponsor programs that might help you.
- **State and local economic development agencies.** Every state has agencies promoting economic development. They recruit new businesses and work to develop and retain existing businesses. You might consult these agencies for advice on state and local loan programs and special tax incentives. Check with your SBDC or local Chamber of Commerce for contact information.

Help from Books and the Internet

Throughout this book, we've listed many book and Internet resources to help you with specific topics. Here's a summary, along with a number of additional sources we like.

Books

Three Favorites

The E-Myth Revisited: Why Most Small Businesses Don't Work and What To Do About It, by Michael E. Gerber (HarperCollins), explains the various roles you must play in your business (entrepreneur, manager, and technician) and shows how to work on your business, not just in your business.

Free Agent Nation: The Future of Working for Yourself, by Daniel H. Pink (Warner Books), demonstrates the growth in the number of self-employed (free agent) Americans and tells how to launch your own free agent business.

The Three Boxes of Life and How to Get Out of Them: An Introduction to Life/Work Planning, by Richard N. Bolles (Ten Speed Press), shows how our lives fall into three phases (education, work, and retirement) and guides the reader through exercises to help achieve balance.

Business Ideas

The 200 Best Home Businesses: Easy to Start, Fun to Run, Highly Profitable, by Katina Jones (Adams Media Corporation), includes the pros and cons of starting different businesses and helps you estimate start-up costs.

Best Home Businesses for People 50+, by Sarah and Paul Edwards (Tarcher), features 70 comprehensive profiles of businesses particularly well-suited for retirees.

101 Internet Businesses You Can Start from Home: How to Choose and Build Your Own Successful e-Business, by Susan Sweeney (Maximum Press), focuses on choosing an online business that you can operate from home.

Comprehensive Business Books

Legal Guide for Starting & Running a Small Business, by Fred S. Steingold (Nolo), covers everything from choosing the right business form and raising start-up funds to getting permits, hiring help, and writing sound business contracts.

Legal Forms for Starting & Running a Small Business, by Fred S. Steingold (Nolo), is a companion to the *Legal Guide*, offering more than 60 forms and documents to help you with your business. The documents include basic contracts, leases, employee agreements, and more.

The Small Business Start-Up Kit, by Peri H. Pakroo (Nolo), shows you how to select the best form of business organization, file the right forms, get the proper licenses and permits, and handle basic record keeping.

The Entrepreneur's Internet Handbook: Your Legal and Practical Guide to Starting a Business Website, by Hugo Barreca and Julia K. O'Neil (Sourcebooks), shows how to set up and maintain a website that is both legal and appealing to customers. It also provides suggestions for drawing visitors to a website.

Six-Week Start-Up: A Step-By-Step Program for Starting Your Business, Making Money, and Achieving Your Goals, by Rhonda Abrams (The Planning Shop), provides a well-organized and easy-to-use approach for getting your business up and running in six weeks.

Sole Proprietorships

Working for Yourself: Law & Taxes for Independent Contractors, Freelancers & Consultants, by Stephen Fishman (Nolo), is a complete resource for those who are self-employed and offering their services on a contract basis. If you will work as an independent contractor, the book shows you how to start your business, handle your taxes, and make sure you get paid what you're worth.

Small Time Operator, by Bernard Kamoroff, CPA (Bell Springs Publishing), is a good source of practical information on getting a sole proprietorship off the ground—from securing a business license, to paying taxes, to handling basic accounting. It includes ledgers and worksheets to get you started.

Partnerships

Form a Partnership: The Complete Legal Guide, by Ralph Warner and Denis Clifford (Nolo), explains the legal and practical issues involved in forming a business partnership, creating a partnership agreement, and protecting each person's interests.

Corporations

Incorporate Your Business: A Legal Guide to Forming a Corporation in Your State, by Anthony Mancuso (Nolo), shows you how to set up and run a corporation in any state.

LLCs

LLC or Corporation? How to Choose the Right Form for Your Business, by Anthony Mancuso (Nolo), provides all the details to help you decide whether an LLC or a corporation is better for your business.

Form Your Own Limited Liability Company, by Anthony Mancuso (Nolo), explains how to set up an LLC in any state, with or without a lawyer's help.

Copyrights, Trademarks, and Patents

The Copyright Handbook: What Every Writer Needs to Know, by Stephen Fishman (Nolo), is a complete guide to copyright rules. It includes forms for registering your copyrights.

Trademark: Legal Care for Your Business & Product Name, by Stephen Elias (Nolo), shows you how to choose a legally strong business and product name, register the name with state and federal agencies, and handle trademark disputes.

Nolo's Patents for Beginners, by David Pressman and Richard Stim (Nolo), provides a thorough overview of what it takes to obtain a patent, including an explanation of how to prepare and file a provisional patent application.

Patent It Yourself, by David Pressman (Nolo), is a complete guide to patent protection, taking you step by step through the process of getting a patent without hiring a patent lawyer.

Leases

Negotiate the Best Lease for Your Business, by Janet Portman and Fred Steingold (Nolo), gives you all the information you need to choose the best location and negotiate a commercial lease.

Employers' Rights and Responsibilities

The Employer's Legal Handbook, by Fred Steingold (Nolo), explains employers' legal rights and responsibilities in detail.

Working With Independent Contractors, by Stephen Fishman (Nolo), shows you how to determine who qualifies as an independent contractor, create valid contracts, and more.

Taxes

Tax Savvy for Small Business, by Frederick Daily (Nolo), provides an in-depth look at federal business taxes and shows small business owners how to make the right tax decisions.

Deduct It! Lower Your Small Business Taxes, by Stephen Fishman (Nolo), provides key information and strategies for keeping your tax bill under control.

Home Business Tax Deductions: Keep What You Earn, by Stephen Fishman (Nolo), is a detailed guide to taxes for small business owners who operate from home.

Financing and Business Plans

Investors in Your Backyard, by Asheesh Advani (Nolo), shows you how to raise start-up money for your business by responsibly approaching family, friends, and other potential supporters.

How to Write a Business Plan, by Mike McKeever (Nolo), is a step by step guide to writing an accurate, effective business plan. *Business Plan Pro* is software by Palo Alto Software, available at www.nolo.com, that helps you do the same thing.

Marketing

Marketing Without Advertising: Inspire Customers to Rave About Your Business & Create Lasting Success, by Michael Phillips, Salli Rasberry, and Diana Fitzpatrick (Nolo), gives practical tips and advice about forming long-lasting relationships with your customers.

Small Business Marketing for Dummies, by Barbara Findlay Schenck (For Dummies), addresses marketing issues in a way that is useful to a new business owner.

The Ultimate Small Business Marketing Toolkit: All the Tips, Forms, and Strategies You'll Ever Need, by Beth Goldstein (McGraw-Hill), contains dozens of worksheets to help you effectively market your new business.

Retirement Planning

Boomer or Bust: Your Financial Guide to Retirement, Health Care, Medicare, and Long-Term Care, by Steve Weisman (Prentice Hall), provides financial guidance about a wide variety of issues that Boomers are facing as they plan their retirement.

The Wall Street Journal Complete Retirement Guidebook: How to Plan It, Live It and Enjoy It, by Glenn Ruffenach and Kelly Greene (Three Rivers Press), includes many stories of retirees finding their way in retirement and helps you tailor a financial plan for the retirement lifestyle you want.

The Motley Fool's Money After 40: Building Wealth for a Better Life, by David and Tom Gardner (Fireside), designed as a "to-do" book not a "how-to-do" book, this book includes numerous action plans to help you strengthen your financial position and organize your finances so you'll have what you need and want in retirement.

You Can Do It!: The Boomer's Guide to a Great Retirement, by Jonathan D. Pond (Collins), proves that it is never too late to start preparing for retirement.

What Color is Your Parachute? for Retirement: Planning Now for the Life You Want, by Richard N. Bolles and John E. Nelson (Ten Speed Press), is a step-by-step guide that helps you prepare for the next stage of life and develop a picture of your ideal retirement.

Other Books About Retirement

Time for Life: The Surprising Ways Americans Use Their Time, by John P. Robinson and Geoffrey Godbey (Pennsylvania State University Press), is a report about how we spend our time based on actual time diaries kept by a wide variety of Americans.

Age Power: How the 21st Century Will Be Ruled by the New Old, by Ken Dychtwald (Tarcher), talks about challenges and solutions we face as the number of Americans over 65 increase dramatically in the next few decades.

Internet Resources

Starting and Running Your Business

Nolo, www.nolo.com. Nolo's website provides answers to a wide variety of legal and practical questions that affect small business owners every day. Check out the "Nolopedia," an extensive library of free articles, FAQs, and tips.

CCH Business Owner's Toolkit, www.toolkit.com. CCH offers more than 5,000 pages of useful—and free—articles and tools for small business owners, including checklists, templates that you can download, and start-up advice.

***Inc.* Magazine, www.inc.com.** Check out the One-Person Business resource center to discover lots of valuable articles, columns, and how-to guides.

Palo Alto Software, www.bplans.com. This website features free expert advice about a variety of business topics and provides over 100 sample business plans.

***Entrepreneur* Magazine, www.entrepreneur.com.** *Entrepreneur* is a good source for business ideas, start-up articles, and information about franchises.

Business Laws & Regulations, www.business.gov. This website is promoted as the official business link to the U.S. government. Use the "Permit Me" feature to help determine which licenses and permits you will need for your business in a given state.

Market Research

Hoover's, www.hoovers.com. Hoover's offers free overviews from their database of more than 24,000,000 companies and more than 600 industries.

BizMiner, www.bizminer.com. BizMiner gives you access to 1,500 free industry financial reports.

Help From the Governement

Small Business Development Centers, www.asbdc-us.org. Enter your zip code and find the closest center, where you can obtain free counseling and low-cost seminars.

SCORE, www.score.org. This site allows you to easily access more than 10,000 volunteer SCORE (Service Corps of Retired Executives) counselors at 389 chapters throughout the United States.

U.S. Small Business Administration, www.sba.gov. This is a helpful place to visit for information about a variety of free government services. The website also offers more than 25 free online courses covering a variety of business topics.

Internal Revenue Service, www.irs.gov. Go to the IRS for tax-related forms and publications, and to apply online for an EIN (Employer Identification Number). You can also click on "Retirement Plans Community" for helpful information about various retirement plans.

Social Security Administration, www.socialsecurity.gov. The official website of the U.S. Social Security Administration.

Medicare, www.medicare.gov. The official U.S. government site for information about Medicare.

Information About Retirement

AARP, www.aarpmagazine.org. AARP is the leading organization for providing information and articles about issues retirees face.

APPENDIX

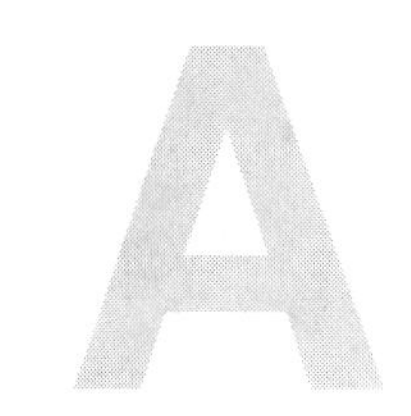

How to Use the CD-ROM

For instructions on using the CD-ROM that accompanies this book, please read this appendix and the README.TXT file included on the CD itself.

CD-ROM Basics

The CD-ROM can be used with Windows computers. It is not a stand-alone software program. The CD installs files that use software programs that need to be on your computer already.

In accordance with U.S. copyright laws, remember that copies of the CD-ROM and its files are for your personal use only.

Two types of files are included on the CD-ROM:

1. **Word processing (RTF) files:** All of the Tools in this book are included on the CD-ROM as RTF files. This means that you can open, complete, print, and save these Tools with your word processing program. (See "Using the Word Processing (RTF) Files to Create Documents," below.) Using the RTF versions of a Tool can be particularly helpful if you want to change a Tool to suit your needs—for example, by adding new categories or more space for your entries.
2. **Portable Document Format (PDF) files.** Each Tool is also available as a PDF file, as are the several bonus items included on the CD-ROM. These files that can be viewed only with Adobe Acrobat Reader. (See "Using Print-Only Files to Complete Your Tools," below.) These PDF Tools are designed to be printed out and filled in by hand or with a typewriter. You won't be able to expand or edit these forms, but you may choose to use them if you want a Tool that has a more professional look.

See the end of this appendix for a list of Tools and bonus items, their file names, and their file formats.

Note to Macintosh Users: This CD-ROM and its files should also work on Macintosh computers. Please note, however, that Nolo cannot provide technical support for non-Windows users.

How to View the README File

To view the Readme.txt file, insert the CD-ROM into your computer's CD-ROM drive and follow these instructions.

Windows 2000, XP, and Vista

(1) On your computer's desktop, double click the My Computer icon; (2) double click the icon for the CD-ROM drive into which you inserted the CD-ROM; (3) double click the Readme.txt file.

Macintosh

(1) On your Mac desktop, double click the icon for the CD-ROM that you inserted and (2) double click the file README.TXT.

While the README file is open, print it out by using the Print command in the File menu.

Installing Files From the CD-ROM Onto Your Computer

To work with the files on the CD-ROM, you first need to install them onto your computer.

Windows 2000, XP, and Vista

Follow the instructions that appear on the screen.

If nothing happens when you insert the CD-ROM, then (1) double click the My Computer icon; (2) double click the icon for the CD-ROM drive into which the CD-ROM was inserted; and (3) double click the file Setup.exe.

Macintosh

If the "Retirement Business CD" window is not open, open it by double clicking the "Retirement Business CD" icon. Then, (1) select the "Retirement Business Forms" folder icon; and (2) drag and drop the folder icon onto your computer.

Where Are the Forms Installed?

Windows 2000, XP, and Vista

All files are installed by default to a folder named \Retirement Business Tools in the \Program Files folder of your computer.

Macintosh

All files are located in the "Retirement Business Tools" folder.

Using the Word Processing (RTF) Files to Complete Your Tools

The files that you can open and edit with your word processing program are in rich text format and include the extension ".RTF." For example, the Tax Checklist discussed in Chapter 13 is the file TaxChecklist.rtf. RTF files can be read by most recent word processing programs including Microsoft *Word*, *WordPad*, and recent versions of Corel *WordPerfect*.

General Instructions for RTF Files

Each word processor uses different commands to open, format, save, and print documents. Please read your word processor's manual for specific instructions on performing these tasks. Do not call Nolo's technical support if you have questions on how to use your word processor or computer.

To use an RTF Tool from the CD-ROM you must: (1) open a file in your word processor or text editor; (2) complete the Tool by filling in the required information; (3) print it out (if you like); and (4) rename and save your revised file.

Opening a File

There are three ways to open the word processing files included on the CD-ROM after you have installed them onto your computer.

1. Windows users can open a file by selecting its "shortcut." (1) Click the Windows "Start" button; (2) open the "Programs" folder; (3) open the "Retirement Business Tools" folder; (4) open the subfolder with the chapter number for the Tools you want or "Your Business Retirement Profile" for the Profile; (5) click the shortcut to the form you want to work with.
2. Both Windows and Macintosh users can open a file directly by double clicking on it. (1) Use My Computer or Windows Explorer (Windows 2000, XP, or Vista) or the Finder (Macintosh) to go to the "Business Retirement Forms" folder; (2) double click the subfolder with the chapter number for the Tool you want or "Your Business Retirement Profile" for the Profile; (3) double click the specific file you want to open.
3. Windows and Macintosh users can open a file from within their word processor. (1) Open the word processor; (2) go to the File menu and choose the "Open" command. This opens a dialog box where (3) you can select the location and name of the file, navigating to the version of the "Retirement Business Tools" folder that you've installed on your computer.

Editing the Tools

Here are tips for working on your Tools.

Underlines indicate where to enter your information, frequently including bracketed instructions. Delete the underlines and instructions before finishing your document.

Some forms have check boxes that appear before text. Check boxes indicate:

- Optional text that you can choose to include or exclude.
- Alternative text that you select to include, excluding the other alternatives.

Optional text

Delete optional text you do not want to include and keep that which you do. In either case, delete the check box and the italicized instructions. If you choose to delete an optional numbered clause, renumber the subsequent clauses after deleting it.

Alternative text

Delete the alternatives that you do not want to include first. Then delete the remaining check boxes, as well as any italicized instructions that you need to select one of the alternatives provided.

Printing a Tool

Use your word processor's or text editor's "Print" command to print out your completed Tools.

Saving Your Document

Use the "Save As" command to save and rename a file. You will be unable to use the "Save" command because the files are "read-only." If you save a file without renaming it, the underlines that indicate where you need to enter your information will be lost and you will not be able to create a new Tool with this file without recopying the original file from the CD-ROM.

Using Print-Only Files to Complete Your Tools

The CD-ROM includes useful forms in Adobe Acrobat PDF format. To use them, you need Adobe Reader installed on your computer. If you don't already have this software, you can download it for free at www .adobe.com.

Opening PDF Files

PDF files, like the word processing files, can be opened one of three ways.

1. Windows users can open a file by selecting its "shortcut." (1) Click the Windows "Start" button; (2) open the "Programs" folder; (3) open the "Retirement Business Tools" folder; (4) open the subfolder for the chapter your tool is in; (5) click the shortcut to the form you want to work with.
2. Both Windows and Macintosh users can open a file directly by double clicking on it. (1) Use My Computer or Windows Explorer (Windows 2000, XP, or Vista) or the Finder (Macintosh) to go to the "Retirement Business Tools" folder; (2) double click the subfolder for the chapter that contains your tool; (3) double click the specific file for the Tool you want to open.
3. Windows and Macintosh users can open a file from within your word processor. (1) Open your word processor; (2) go to the "File" menu and choose the "Open" command. This opens a dialog box where (3) you will select the location and name of the file, navigating to the version of the "Retirement Business Tools" folder that you've installed on your computer.

Filling in PDF Files

The PDF files cannot be filled out using your computer. To complete a Tool using one of these files, print it out and then complete it by hand or typewriter.

Money Tools: Using the *Excel* Spreadsheets

The following guidelines will help you use the Excel versions of the Money Tools contained in Chapter 6.

General Instructions for Money Tools

Open the file MoneyTools.xls on the CD-ROM using *Excel.* There are nine worksheets in the file; seven of them call for you to type in your financial data. The name of each worksheet is on the tab at the bottom of the page. (If you can't see all of the tabs at once, use the arrows in the lower left corner to scroll through the worksheets.)

The first two worksheets have features that help you test different scenarios for drawing monthly income during retirement. These two worksheets are called:

- Retirement Plans, and
- Liquid Assets.

The next five worksheets ask for the same information as the Tools in Chapter 6 of this book, but they calculate your totals automatically. These five worksheets are called:

- Real Estate
- Collectibles
- Toys and Necessities
- Other Liabilities, and
- Retirement Living Expenses.

The last two worksheets summarize the first seven and require no action on your part. These worksheets are labeled:

- Financial Summary, and
- Financial Details.

Entering Data

The instructions in this section apply to the seven worksheets that require you to enter data:

- **Green cells:** You can change the information in any cell that is shaded green; these cells are where you enter your financial information. Note that you can modify a green cell that contains a label. In these cells, we have provided standard lists of assets, liabilities, and expenses as a starting point, but you can change them to suit your needs or add to them if necessary.
- **Yellow cells:** You can't change the information in a cell that is shaded yellow; these cells contain formulas or labels that are necessary to make the worksheets function correctly. "N/A" indicates that cell is not applicable for the item in that row. The Tool will automatically calculate the figures for all yellow cells.
- **Account balance or market value:** You will be asked to provide the account balance or market value of your assets as of the day you plan to retire. Start with your current balances or values and adjust to reflect your plans and assumptions about changes in the economy.
- **Entering dollar amounts:** All dollar amounts will be displayed with a "$" sign and will be rounded to the nearest dollar. We encourage you to round all of your entries to the nearest $100; this level of accuracy is sufficient for making your projections.
- **Column references:** The instructions for entering figures (below) indicate the column letter as well as the name of the column where you will enter the data. Note that Column A is used as a border for printed reports and Column B contains row labels. You will begin the first six worksheets by entering account balance or market value information in Column C. For the Retirement Living Expenses worksheet you will use your present living expenses as a starting point in Column C.

Retirement Plans

This worksheet helps you determine the monthly income you can anticipate from your retirement plans. It is divided into two sections:

Retirement Plans Tool. In Columns C and D, enter the projected account balance and monthly income for each of your retirement plans. These two columns are the same as the Tool in Chapter 6. You can get the monthly income for Column D either by talking with your plan administrator or financial adviser, or by using the next portion of the worksheet: the Monthly Income Calculator.

Monthly Income Calculator. This side of the worksheet can help you calculate an amount to enter in Column D. You can experiment with different earnings rates, number of years, and amount of cushion you'd like to keep in each account. Each time, a new monthly retirement income amount will be calculated for you in Column J. Experiment as much as you like, then choose an amount to enter into Column D.

EXAMPLE: Let's say you have $135,000 in an IRA account. You want to keep a cushion of $25,000 in the account, and you project that your IRA will earn 7% per year as you withdraw funds over a period of 25 years. The Monthly Income Calculator will show that this will provide you with $949 per month. If you change the earnings rate to 8%, your monthly retirement income increases to $1,035. You can continue to work with the Calculator until you're comfortable choosing an amount to enter in Column D—in our example, that might be $1,000 per month.

We suggest that you proceed through the columns in the order listed here:

- **Projected Account Balance at Retirement (Column C).** Estimate the balance in each of your retirement plans, except Social Security, when you retire.
- **Desired Account Balance Cushion (Column F).** For each retirement account, enter the minimum balance you want to maintain. This is called your cushion or reserve. Your cushion is the amount of money that makes you feel comfortable and free from worries about running

out of money. Entering an amount in this column will cause an automatic calculation of your "Funds Available for Monthly Income" in Column G.

- **Anticipated Annual Earnings Rate (Column H).** Decide the expected rate of return for your retirement plans and enter the percentage. For example, enter 8.2% as 8.2.
- **Number of Years of Monthly Income (Column I).** Select the number of years you will withdraw monthly retirement income from each plan. Most people base this decision on their life expectancy after they have retired but you may decide to take the money out of some retirement accounts faster than others. Entering the number of years will cause automatic calculation of your "Calculated Estimate of Monthly Income" in Column J.
- **Projected Monthly Income in Retirement (Column D).** Input your projected monthly income. For defined benefits plans, use information from your retirement plan administrator. For Social Security, use information from the Social Security Administration. For all other retirement plans, make your entries based on the figures in Column J or information from your financial planner.

Liquid Assets

The liquid assets worksheet helps you calculate the monthly income you can draw from your liquid assets during retirement. It is divided into two sections, just like the one for retirement plans.

Liquid Assets Tool. In Columns C and D, enter the projected account balance and monthly income for each of your liquid assets. These two columns are the same as the Tool in Chapter 6. You can get the monthly income for Column D either by talking with your financial adviser or by using the next portion of the worksheet: the Monthly Income Calculator.

Monthly Income Calculator. This side of the worksheet can help you calculate an amount to enter in Column D. You can experiment with different earnings rates, number of years, and amount of cushion you'd like to keep in each account. Each time, a new monthly income amount will be calculated for you in Column J. Experiment as much as you like, then choose an amount to enter into Column D.

We suggest that you proceed through the columns in the order listed here:

- **Projected Account Balance at Retirement (Column C).** Estimate the balance in each of your liquid asset accounts when you retire.
- **Desired Account Balance Cushion (Column F).** For each account, enter the minimum balance you want to maintain. This is called your cushion or reserve. These funds will help you pay for unplanned expenses, such as medical bills or a broken washing machine. Your cushion is also the amount of money that makes you feel comfortable, free from worries about running out of money. Some retirees never reduce their investment principal; their monthly retirement income is just what they earn on their investments. If that's your plan, make your cushion equal to your total liquid assets when you retire. You will see an automatic calculation of your "Funds Available for Monthly Income" in Column G.
- **Anticipated Annual Earnings Rate (Column H).** Decide the expected rate of return for your liquid assets and enter the percentage. For example, enter 6.3% as 6.3.
- **Number of Years of Monthly Income (Column I).** Select the number of years you will take your liquid assets as monthly retirement income. You are choosing the number of years that reduces your liquid assets to your cushion amount. Most people base this decision on their life expectancy after they have retired.
- **Projected Monthly Income in Retirement (Column D).** Make your entries based on the figures in Column J or from information provided by your financial planner.

Real Estate

The worksheet for real estate has the same four columns as the Tool in Chapter 6. Projected Equity and Projected Net Cash Flow at the bottom of the worksheet are calculated for you. Remember:

Total Projected Market Value at Retirement
– Total Loan Balance at Retirement
= Projected Equity

Total Monthly Income in Retirement
– Total Monthly Expenses in Retirement
= Projected Net Cash Flow

Enter the following information for each item:

- **Projected Market Value at Retirement (Column C).** Estimate what each piece of real estate will be worth when you retire.
- **Projected Loan Balance at Retirement (Column D).** Estimate the balance of any loan you will have on each asset when you retire.
- **Projected Monthly Income in Retirement (Column E).** Make your entries based on the income you plan to earn when you retire. Remember that this does not apply to your primary home, so it has been marked "N/A."
- **Projected Monthly Expenses in Retirement (Column F).** Make your entries based on your present monthly expenses adjusted for expected inflation.

Collectibles

The worksheet for collectibles and other income-producing assets has the same two columns as the Tool in Chapter 6. It requires you to enter the following information for each item:

- **Projected Market Value at Retirement (Column C).** Estimate what each asset will be worth when you retire.

- **Projected Monthly Income in Retirement (Column D).** Make your entries based on your plans for each of these assets.

Toys and Necessities

The worksheet for toys and necessities contains the same columns as the Tool in Chapter 6. Enter the following information for each item:

- **Projected Market Value at Retirement (Column C).** Estimate what each asset will be worth when you retire.
- **Projected Loan Balance at Retirement (Column D).** Estimate the balance of any loan you will have on each asset when you retire.
- **Projected Monthly Payment in Retirement (Column E).** Make your entries based on your plans for each asset.

Other Liabilities

This worksheet has the same two columns as the Tool in Chapter 6. Enter the following information for each item:

- **Projected Amount Owed at Retirement (Column C).** Estimate the amount you will owe on each debt when you retire.
- **Projected Monthly Payment in Retirement (Column D).** Make your entries based on your plans for each debt.

Retirement Living Expenses

The worksheet for living expenses is the same as the Tool in Chapter 6. Enter the following information for each item:

- **Estimated Present Monthly Expenses (Column C).** Estimate your present monthly living expenses for each item.
- **Projected Monthly Expenses in Retirement (Column E).** Make your entries based on your best guesses for your retirement living expenses. Be sure to account for inflation.

Completing the Summary Worksheets

The Financial Summary and Financial Details worksheets are produced automatically. Take a minute to review the figures on these two worksheets.

Financial Summary Worksheet. The Financial Summary worksheet is a brief summary of the previous seven worksheets. Review the worksheet to see if the figures make sense. If the figures seem wrong, check the next worksheet.

Financial Details Worksheet. The Financial Details worksheet is a detailed listing of all the line items from the seven Tools in this chapter. This listing is very helpful for identifying errors.

Printing Worksheets

It is often easier to verify the accuracy of the data you have entered if you have a printed copy of the worksheet in front of you. You have two options for printing your worksheets:

- **Print a single worksheet.** In the Print dialog box select "Active sheet(s)." The worksheet you have been working on will print.
- **Print all nine worksheets.** In the Print dialog box select "Entire workbook." All nine worksheets will print.

Each printed worksheet will be in the same format as the corresponding Tool in the Chapter 6, except for "Financial Details," which is a special feature contained only on the CD-ROM.

Files on the CD-ROM

Files in RTF Format	
Jumpstart Your Thinking	Jumpstart.rtf
If You Could Do Anything	DoAnything.rtf
Your Key Interests	KeyInterests.rtf
Your Retirement Goals	RetirementGoals.rtf
Your Goal Statements	GoalStatements.rtf
Your Motivation	Motivation.rtf
Your Values Inventory	ValueInventory.rtf
Your Key Values	KeyValues.rtf
Your Work Style	WorkStyles.rtf
You and Your Money	Money.rtf
Move or Stay?	Move.rtf
Factors to Consider When You Move	MoveFactors.rtf
Your Key Factors	KeyFactors.rtf
Your Worker Skills	WorkerSkills.rtf
Your Owner Skills	OwnerSkills.rtf
Your Typical Year	TypicalYear.rtf
Your Work Time	WorkTime.rtf
Time for Yourself	TimeforYourself.rtf
Time for Obligations	TimeforObligations.rtf
Your 168 Hours	168hours.rtf
Your Retirement Plans	RetirementPlans.rtf
Your Liquid Assets	LiquidAssets.rtf
Your Real Estate	RealEstate.rtf
Your Collectibles and Other Assets	Collectibles.rtf
Your Toys and Necessities	Necessities.rtf

Files in RTF Format, continued	
Your Other Liabilities	Liabilities.rtf
Your Retirement Living Expenses	LivingExpenses.rtf
Your Financial Summary	FinancialSummary.rtf
Business Idea Cards	IdeaCards.rtf
Ideas From Your Employment	IdeasEmployment.rtf
Ideas From Your Interests	IdeasInterest.rtf
Ideas From Your Skills	IdeasSkill.rtf
Ideas From Your Consumer Experiences	IdeasExperiences.rtf
Ideas From Copycatting	IdeasCopycatting.rtf
Ideas From Evaluating Trends	IdeasTrends.rtf
Your Number One Business Idea	BusinessIdea.rtf
Your Monthly Fixed Costs	MonthlyFixedCosts.rtf
Your Variable Costs	VariableCosts.rtf
Your Contribution Margin	ContributionMargin.rtf
Customers Needed to Meet Your Financial Goals	CustomersNeeded.rtf
Capacity to Serve Your Customers	CapacityCustomers.rtf
Evaluating Your Competition	Competition.rtf
Your Start-Up Costs	StartUpCosts.rtf
Your Working Capital	WorkingCapital.rtf
Ability to Finance Your Business Idea	AbilityToFinance.rtf
Legal Tasks and Decisions	Legal.rtf
Financing Your Business	Financing.rtf
Tax Checklist	TaxChecklist.rtf
Health Insurance Checklist	InsuranceChecklist.rtf
Your Retirement Business Profile	Profile.rtf

Files in PDF Format	
Jumpstart Your Thinking	Jumpstart.pdf
If You Could Do Anything	DoAnything.pdf
Your Key Interests	KeyInterests.pdf
Your Retirement Goals	RetirementGoals.pdf
Your Goal Statements	GoalStatements.pdf
Your Motivation	Motivation.pdf
Your Values Inventory	ValueInventory.pdf
Your Key Values	KeyValues.pdf
Your Work Style	WorkStyles.pdf
You and Your Money	Money.pdf
Move or Stay?	Move.pdf
Factors to Consider When You Move	MoveFactors.pdf
Your Key Factors	KeyFactors.pdf
Your Worker Skills	WorkerSkills.pdf
Your Owner Skills	OwnerSkills.pdf
Your Typical Year	TypicalYear.pdf
Your Work Time	WorkTime.pdf
Time for Yourself	TimeforYourself.pdf
Time for Obligations	TimeforObligations.pdf
Your 168 Hours	168hours.pdf
Your Retirement Plans	RetirementPlans.pdf
Your Liquid Assets	LiquidAssets.pdf
Your Real Estate	RealEstate.pdf
Your Collectibles and Other Assets	Collectibles.pdf
Your Toys and Necessities	Necessities.pdf
Your Other Liabilities	Liabilities.pdf
Your Retirement Living Expenses	LivingExpenses.pdf
Your Financial Summary	FinancialSummary.pdf

Files in PDF Format, continued	
Business Idea Cards	IdeaCards.pdf
Ideas From Your Employment	IdeasEmployment.pdf
Ideas From Your Interests	IdeasInterest.pdf
Ideas From Your Skills	IdeasSkill.pdf
Ideas From Your Consumer Experiences	IdeasExperiences.pdf
Ideas From Copycatting	IdeasCopycatting.pdf
Ideas From Evaluating Trends	IdeasTrends.pdf
Your Number One Business Idea	BusinessIdea.pdf
Your Monthly Fixed Costs	MonthlyFixedCosts.pdf
Your Variable Costs	VariableCosts.pdf
Your Contribution Margin	ContributionMargin.pdf
Customers Needed to Meet Your Financial Goals	CustomersNeeded.pdf
Capacity to Serve Your Customers	CapacityCustomers.pdf
Evaluating Your Competition	Competition.pdf
Your Start-Up Costs	StartUpCosts.pdf
Your Working Capital	WorkingCapital.pdf
Ability to Finance Your Business Idea	AbilityToFinance.pdf
Legal Tasks and Decisions	Legal.pdf
Financing Your Business	Financing.pdf
Tax Checklist	TaxChecklist.pdf
Health Insurance Checklist	InsuranceChecklist.pdf
Accomplish Your Goals With an Action Plan Skills, Time, and Money Your Action Plan	ActionPlan.pdf
Fill Your Skills Gaps Your Business Tasks Handling Worker Tasks Handling Owner Tasks	Gap.pdf

Files in PDF Format, continued	
Is Selling Online Right for Your Business? Should You Sell Online?	Online.pdf
Write Your Elevator Speech Your Customers' Attributes Your Customers' Wants and Needs Your Elevator Speech	Elevator.pdf

Worksheets in XLS Format
The following worksheets are found in the MoneyTools.xls file:
Retirement Plans
Liquid Assets
Real Estate
Collectibles
Toys and Necessities
Other Liabilities
Retirement Living Expenses
Financial Summary Worksheet
Financial Details Worksheet

APPENDIX

Your Retirement Business Profile

Interests

It is an absolute must that my business be centered on my interest in ________________
____.

It is important that my business be related to my interest in ________________________,
___________________________________ but that does not have to be the central focus.

It would be nice, but not necessary, if my business involves my interest in _____________
____.

Additional statements about my interests:

____

____

____

Goals

I want to balance the following retirement goals with my goal of starting a business:

____

____

____

Additional statements about my goals:

____

____

____

Motivations

My primary motivation for starting a business in retirement is ______________________,
________________ so it is very important that my business allows me to accomplish this.

I also have the following motivation for starting a business in retirement: _____________
___________ so it is somewhat important that my business allows me to accomplish this.

Additional statements about my motivations for starting a business:

____

____

____

Values

List a value here:	It is very important that my business be centered on this value.	I would like my business to reflect this value, but it doesn't have to be the main focus.	It is very important that my retirement business not conflict with this value.	This value need not be reflected in my retirement business. I will address it in other aspects of my life.

Additional statements about my values:

____

____

____

Work Style

I would enjoy a business with: (check all that apply)

- ❑ lots of contact with people whom I get to know really well
- ❑ very little contact with people
- ❑ some contact with people, but time spent alone, too
- ❑ lots of contact with people, but on a casual basis that doesn't require me to get too involved with them
- ❑ lots of networking required to get new customers

- ❑ very little networking required to get new customers
- ❑ some networking, but mostly with people I already know
- ❑ many opportunities to talk to people
- ❑ little requirement to talk to people

Additional statements about social contact in my business:

____

____

____

Typically, I: (check all that apply)

- ❑ avoid change, so my business should not stray far from what I already know or do
- ❑ thrive on change, so I'd love my business to be in a field totally new to me
- ❑ need time to ease into change, so I'd prefer a slow transition into my retirement business
- ❑ dive right into new things, so I'd prefer quick entry into my retirement business

Additional statements about change, transition, and my retirement business:

____

____

____

My ideal retirement business would include this balance:

______% **Big-picture work** (determining direction, building strategies and relationships, helping customers find solutions, tackling challenging problems, seeking new opportunities)

______% **Detail work** (record keeping, organizing papers and files, monitoring deadlines, keeping customers on track)

Additional statements about the type of work I want to do in my retirement business:

___

___

___

Attitude About Money

I am comfortable risking this much of my savings in my retirement business (check one):

❑ none

❑ a small amount

❑ quite a bit

If it takes more money to start my business than I can invest (check one):

❑ I will be comfortable borrowing money.

❑ I will not be comfortable borrowing money.

I will measure the success of my business mainly by the amount of money I earn.

❑ yes ❑ no

Additional statements about my attitude toward money:

___

___

___

Location

I plan to live in ___ so my business must be feasible there.

I plan to snowbird, spending ___ months in ___ and ___ months in ___, so my business either has to travel with me or be seasonal.

I plan to travel ___ months per year in my RV, so my business either has to travel with me or be seasonal.

I'm not clear where I want to live, but I will probably start out in ___ .

It's possible I will move around a bit in retirement, so my business needs to be portable.

❑ yes ❑ no

Additional statements about where I plan to live:

____

____

____.

Skills

In my worker role, I can use the following skills to serve my customers:

____

____

____.

In my owner role, I can use the following skills to run my business:

____

____

____.

Every business owner must balance the two roles. Estimate the percentage of time you would like to devote to each role: ______________________________

Worker_____% Owner_____%

Additional statements about my skills:

____

____

____.

Time

I plan to spend _______ weeks per year working on my business.

I would like to spend _______ hours per week working on my business.

I am willing to work nights

❑ yes ❑ no

I am willing to work weekends

❑ yes ❑ no

I prefer: (check one)

❑ set work hours ❑ a flexible work schedule

I prefer: (check one)

❑ working year round ❑ seasonal work

Additional statements about the time I want to spend on my business:

____

____

____.

Financial Guidelines

The most I can invest to start my business is $_______________.

I am comfortable investing $_______________ to start my business.

I must earn at least $_______________ per month during retirement.

I would like to earn $_______________ per month during retirement.

Additional statements about financial guidelines:

____

____

____.

Index

D

E

F

Get the Latest in the Law

Nolo's Legal Updater

We'll send you an email whenever a new edition of your book is published! Sign up at **www.nolo.com/legalupdater**.

Updates at Nolo.com

Check **www.nolo.com/update** to find recent changes in the law that affect the current edition of your book.

Nolo Customer Service

To make sure that this edition of the book is the most recent one, call us at **800-728-3555** and ask one of our friendly customer service representatives (7:00 am to 6:00 pm PST, weekdays only). Or find out at **www.nolo.com**.

Complete the Registration & Comment Card ...

... and we'll do the work for you! Just indicate your preferences below:

Registration & Comment Card

NAME ________________________________ DATE __________

ADDRESS ________________________________

CITY ________________ STATE __________ ZIP __________

PHONE ________________ EMAIL ________________

COMMENTS ________________________________

WAS THIS BOOK EASY TO USE? (VERY EASY) 5 4 3 2 1 (VERY DIFFICULT)

☐ Yes, you can quote me in future Nolo promotional materials. *Please include phone number above.*

☐ Yes, send me **Nolo's Legal Updater** via email when a new edition of this book is available.

Yes, I want to sign up for the following email newsletters:

- ☐ **NoloBriefs** (monthly)
- ☐ **Nolo's Special Offer** (monthly)
- ☐ **Nolo's BizBriefs** (monthly)
- ☐ **Every Landlord's Quarterly** (four times a year)

BOSS1

☐ Yes, you can give my contact info to carefully selected partners whose products may be of interest to me.

NOLO

Send to: **Nolo** 950 Parker Street Berkeley, CA 94710-9867, Fax: (800) 645-0895, or include all of the above information in an email to cs@nolo.com with the subject line "BOSS1."